BERKSHIRE N

Other counties in this series include:

BERKSHIRE MURDERS

Ian McLoughlin

COUNTRYSIDE BOOKS
NEWBURY, BERKSHIRE

First Published 1992
© Ian McLoughlin 1992

COUNTRYSIDE BOOKS
3 Catherine Road
Newbury, Berkshire

ISBN 1 85306 195 6

Cover design by Mon Mohan

Produced through MRM Associates Ltd, Reading
Typeset by Paragon Typesetters, Queensferry
Printed by J W Arrowsmith Ltd, Bristol

This book is dedicated to the
hard-working men and women
of Thames Valley Police

Acknowledgements

I would like to acknowledge the considerable help I received from a number of sources in researching this book, especially Thames Valley Police, who made their archives and museum available; Chief Inspector Bill Indge (retd), author of the *History of the Berkshire Constabulary*, for his invaluable assistance; Brian Bailey, author of *Hangmen of England*; the governor and staff of Reading Prison, for their unstinting co-operation (and letting me out again); the *Newbury Weekly News*, especially Jennie Jackson, librarian, and Penelope Stokes, columnist; the *Maidenhead Advertiser*, especially Michelle Harris and Luke Over, the *Berkshire Chronicle*; the *Reading Mercury*; Reading Central Library, especially Margaret Smith; Newbury Library; Linda Barker, of *The Sun*, for her help in researching it, and Nigel Morgan, of the *Newbury Weekly News*, for pestering me to write it. Most of all, my thanks to Malcolm Howe, editor of the *Newbury Advertiser*, for letting me run riot across his pages with tales of murder and mayhem.

Ian McLoughlin
Autumn 1992

Contents

WINDSOR BOROUGH POLICE.

Regulations to be observed by the Constables residing at the Station.

1. Constables are not permitted to remain out of the station after half-past eleven o'clock at night (except when on duty) without leave of the Chief Constable. The roll is to be called at that hour, and every man absent without permission is to be reported by the Officer on duty.

2. All electric lights are to be extinguished by midnight and Officers in bed. No Constable shall be permitted to burn electric light in his room while in bed (except in cases of sickness), and all lights must be turned off when Constables leave their rooms for duty or other purposes. Lights must not be left burning in the kitchen, lavatories, closets, and day room when not occupied.

3. The bedroom windows must be opened whenever circumstances permit, and cleaned as often as required.

4. Day and Night Constables must have their beds made and rooms in order and ventilated by 4 p.m. Articles must not be left lying about, but everything placed in a neat and uniform style (except in case of sickness).

5. Smoking in bedrooms is strictly forbidden, and lamps or candles will not be allowed to be taken into them on any pretext whatever.

6. Clothing and accoutrements must not be cleaned in the bedrooms or dayrooms, all cleaning of uniform, boots, &c., must be done downstairs in the room provided for that purpose.

7. The clothing and accoutrements of each Constable must be placed in the rooms and cupboards set apart for that purpose, and when not in use must be put away in a cleanly state. Boots are at all times to be left downstairs.

8. Each Constable must appear dressed and cleanly at meals every day, and provide himself with a pair of slippers.

9. Each Constable must change his linen and take a bath at least once a week, as there is nothing more conducive to health than regular ablution and clean clothes of every description.

10. Constables must not leave water running in the lavatories or bathroom.

11. No females, whether relatives or friends, will be allowed to enter the Section House without the express permission of the Officer on duty.

12. Bedroom doors are never to be locked or fastened from the inside, and only Police Officers are allowed in the rooms.

13. Constables on night duty must retire to rest half an hour after coming off duty, unless allowed by the Officer on duty to leave the Station for a proper and reasonable purpose.

14. No single Constable is allowed to sleep out of the Section House at any time without the permission of the Chief Constable.

15. Gambling prohibited. Every species of gambling is strictly prohibited in the Station.

16. All utensils, bedclothing, or fixtures damaged or destroyed to be paid for by those damaging the same. All cases of damage, whether accidental or malicious, is to be reported immediately to the Chief Constable on a proper report form.

17. Swearing, profane or obscene language or other immoral or indecent conduct will not be tolerated in the Station.

18. Each Constable has to pay 1s. per week for his lodging, which is deducted from his pay.

The Officer on duty in the Station for the time being will be held responsible for the observance of the foregoing regulations, and any infringement must be reported to the Chief Constable.

BY ORDER OF THE WATCH COMMITTEE.

December 4th, 1907.

Foreword

What is so fascinating about murder that makes our ears prick up and our senses quicken? We shall probably never know. Newspapers go into minute details in their reports, and murder mysteries are hugely popular in novels, films and television series. Since time immemorial, humankind has had a grim fascination with killing – particularly of the unjustified kind – and the retribution attempted by the aggrieved families and friends.

Socio-religious codes have been remarkably successful for thousands of years in keeping murder to a minimum. Most killings are the result of loss of control by the killer. Very few murders are cold-bloodedly planned and callously carried out – contrary to popular myth.

The Royal County of Berkshire has had its fair share of gruesome murders. Their perpetrators range from evil to pathetic but they all had their reasons for killing, and paid the ultimate price for it. I hope you will find their stories interesting.

Ian McLoughlin
Autumn 1992

THE GRUESOME GIBBET
OF COMBE

COMBE Gibbet, on the highest point of the Berkshire-Hampshire border, stands as a grim reminder of the brutality of life in days gone by, and of what wrongdoers could expect if they were caught. Hanging was still the penalty for even minor crimes like sheep-stealing when it was first erected.

In the 17th century George Broomham, a small farmer at West Woodhay, formed a dalliance with a widow, Dorothy Newman, who lived at Combe. The only problem was that he already had a wife. Divorce in those days was impossible for ordinary people, and was rare even among the nobility. The only way Broomham could get rid of his wife Martha was to murder her, and he set to thinking of a way to commit the perfect crime.

One day, on the way home from the fields, he found a wasps' nest. He walked on, slowly homewards, a horrible and highly original idea forming in his mind. A few days later, Broomham and his wife were on their way to market. He said conversationally that he had seen a wasps' nest over there a few days previously. He pointed to some bushes on the windy hillside and stopped his pony and trap near the spot. Mrs Broomham's curiosity was aroused, and she stepped down from the cart. Her husband pulled on a pair of thick leather gauntlets and tied the reins to a bush. She walked up to the nest and looked at the insects flying in and out of the entrance hole. Broomham moved quietly behind her as she watched the busy insects about their business. She was oblivious to her husband's presence as he grabbed her from behind and pushed her head into the nest. It all happened so quickly she barely had time to utter a scream. The angry insects buzzed furiously. The woman struggled vainly for a few seconds, but Broomham kept her in a vice-like grip. She slumped down, the victim of a vastly unequal struggle, her face and neck bloated with stings, as the death rattle came painfully from her throat.

Broomham walked quickly back to the pony and cart, took off his gloves and casually picked up the reins. The pony walked on, and Broomham looked nonchalantly around him as if nothing in the world had happened. The whole village went into mourning when Mrs Broomham's body was found. An apparently distraught Mr Broomham was inconsolable, as grief-stricken neighbours called to pay their respects.

He had got away with it. With his wife's death accepted as a tragic accident, Broomham slipped quietly away to visit the widow at Combe. But he could not resist telling her the gory details of his terrible deed, and they sat in the widow's tiny cottage discussing their plans. Unbeknown to them, the widow's son was in the next room, and heard every word. He was supposed to be asleep, and Broomham opened the door to check. The boy pretended to be sleeping – a ploy which probably saved his life.

Next day he went to the authorities and told them what he had heard while pretending to be asleep. The game was up for Broomham, he was arrested and taken to Winchester prison to await trial.

Combe Gibbet (photograph by Peter Bloodworth).

He was convicted at Winchester Assizes on February 23rd 1676, in the reign of King Charles II. The records of the trial say that as the judge put on his black cap, he said 'Ye are ordered to be hanged in chaynes neere to the place of the murder.'

The judge's order gave the villages of Combe and Inkpen a problem. The murder was committed on the boundary between the two parishes. It was in open countryside at the top of a hill, and there was not a tree large enough to use as a gallows. The court's order meant a gibbet would have to be built. Parish boundary squabbles are usually about claiming territory − not relinquishing it. But both said the spot where the deed was committed was not in their bounds. A sort of no man's land appeared between the two parishes, and each of the two villages claimed the other was responsible for the expense. An unseemly squabble broke out over who would pay. Eventually, pressure from the court forced them to compromise and erect Combe Gibbet at the site of a stone age long barrow at the top of Inkpen Hill.

The sentence was carried out on George Broomham, and his body was left in chains, swinging from the gibbet, his bleached bones a deterrent to others.

The wooden post rotted away as the years went by and was replaced with another. That was struck and split asunder by lightning, and treasure hunters carried off the fragments to make snuff boxes and souvenirs. The third gibbet went up in 1816 and lasted until it was blown down by high winds in 1949. The local paper recorded 'Last Saturday night, it fought out its last battle all alone in the rain and wind. On Sunday morning it was stretched out on the turf.'

Local people subscribed to replace it. The 31 foot length of oak beam was cut from a tree at Inkpen and taken to the site. Labourers dug a seven foot hole and a crane stood by to locate the huge piece of timber in the ground. A written history of the gibbet was placed in a glass tube and inserted in a hole drilled at the base. The BBC was there to record the event for a radio broadcast.

No-one has met their end on the present gibbet, although it has been used several times for publicity stunts, one of the most notable being an anti-poll tax demonstration with a 'body' left hanging from the cross bar in April 1990.

The previous gibbet saw a little more action. American soldiers were thought to have hung an effigy of Adolf Hitler from its crossbar in 1944, and the German Luftwaffe nearly got revenge later that year when a 'doodlebug' flying bomb flew perilously close.

Years later, the story of how Hitler came to be hanging from Combe Gibbet was revealed. Amongst the papers of the late Dr Donald Brown was found a copy of a letter to the chairman of the committee responsible for erecting the fourth gibbet. It read 'I enclose a cheque from myself and in memory of the late Keith Turner. A group of us boys made an effigy of Hitler and hung him from the gibbet one night. We did not damage the old post, which was leaning and shaky. We formed a human pyramid by climbing on each other's shoulders. We are scattered now, and Keith Turner was killed flying over Germany later in the war.'

The old post withstood numerous vandal attacks, but towards the end of 1991 it was burnt down with, according to the police, an oxy-acetylene torch. The reason for the attack is not known, and the perpetrators have never been caught.

The windswept landscape is a strange and eerie place to this day. Rumour has it that Roman soldiers retreating before the invading hordes from Northern Europe buried hundreds of gold coins there, but nothing has ever been found.

HANGED IN CHAINS

ROBBERS and footpads have been attacking helpless victims since time immemorial, and in the summer of 1787 at Padworth two such young villains stalked an old man as he walked slowly across Padworth Common, on his way home to Ufton Nervet. William Billimore had lived in Ufton all his life, but even in his declining years he made the effort to get out and about. The two teenagers waited for the old man to reach a clump of bushes, where he would be out of sight in the unlikely event of anyone being in the woods and seeing the bloody deed that was about to take place. They crept up behind him and beat him senseless with their wooden clubs. The only thing the old man had worth stealing was an old silver pocket watch, his one and only prized possession. The thieves snatched it from his waistcoat and ran off, leaving the old man to die of the horrific wounds inflicted by the heavy cudgels.

The two lived nearby and went home to plan the disposal of their ill-gotten plunder. A silver watch would fetch a pretty penny at a time when many working men were on the brink of starvation. England had been at war for years, and many ordinary people could barely afford the price of a loaf. Riots broke out in several Berkshire towns because of the high price of bread.

Abraham Tull was 19 years old, William Hawkins was only 17. While they discussed their plans to dispose of the watch, the hue and cry went up as the old man's body was found. The whole village turned out to find the killers, and suspicion pointed towards the two youths Tull and Hawkins, who had lost their nerve and fled. The callous murder of William Billimore shocked the whole county. News of the old man's death spread quickly, along with the manhunt for Tull and Hawkins. They were found at Maidenhead, arrested and taken before the magistrates. They were committed for trial at Berkshire Assizes and locked up in jail.

Both pleaded guilty to the murder of William Billimore and the judge put on his black cap to pronounce sentence of death. They were to be hanged in chains at the place where the crime was committed, and their bodies left on the gallows as a grim warning to other criminals.

A gibbet was erected on the road from Padworth Common to Burghfield, on the corner of the road to Mortimer. Hawkins and Tull were taken there and wrapped in the lengths of heavy chain which would keep their skeletons intact once their bodies had decomposed. The sentence was carried out with a large crowd of curious onlookers watching with grisly fascination. The hanging took place within sight of the two men's homes. Their bleached bones, still chained up, swung on the gallows for years afterwards. Rumour had it that the touch of a dead man's hand could cure all sorts of ailments, and it was not uncommon to see afflicted people approach a gibbet to try and touch its victim's hand. The theory was, the fresher the felon's corpse, the more efficacious the remedy. There were even quack doctors who sold 'essence of dead man's hand' at country markets.

Both families bore the disgrace of their black sheep with forbearance. The Tull family, many members of which still live in the county, prefers to remember its more famous son,

Jethro, who invented the horse-hoe and the seed drill which revolutionised planting. One of the latest generations of Tulls is a press photographer in Newbury.

The local people got used to the grim sight and sound of the skeletons in their rattling chains, but a local landowner's wife found their presence objectionable. She arranged for the bodies to be taken down and decently buried. The chains were removed and sent to Reading Museum. The lady's name was Mrs Brocas of Beaurepaire, who lived at nearby Wokefield Park. Brocas Lands Farm exists to this day, near Mortimer, and Beaurepaire Farm is still there, near Padworth Common. The gibbet on the corner of the road to Mortimer is long gone, but local people referred to the site as 'Gibbet Piece' well into this century, and it was thus marked on the Ordnance Survey maps. The land was dug for gravel some years ago, and no trace is left now, not even a ghostly rattle of chains on a windy night.

STAND AND DELIVER!

IN the late 18th century Mr Dormer, a respectable builder in High Wycombe had a son who he named James. He was brought up in this good family and taught the ways of thrift and honesty. He was apprenticed to a bricklayer, a good trade, but the only talent he showed was for laziness and thieving. In fact he was a thoroughly bad lot. In desperation, his family persuaded him to take the King's shilling and join up in the marines, thinking a soldier's life would be the making of him.

They were wrong. Dormer deserted and took up armed robbery. He roamed around the countryside, from ale house to ale house, stealing whatever he could to keep himself in beer money. In the winter of 1800, aged 22, he met Richard Alder, another petty criminal, and the two fell to wondering about the profitability of highway robbery.

The glamorous image of the highwayman appealed to them both. The idea of a tall, masked man astride a black horse, pistols at the ready, was a heady dream for the two young men in rags with no money and little prospect of any future. In reality, their chances of pulling off a stagecoach robbery were probably zero. The coaching companies had learnt to fend off highwaymen, and employed very tough guards, armed to the teeth with the latest weaponry.

Undeterred, the two decided to embark on their new career, and in February, 1801, Alder called for Dormer to join him the following day to try their luck. Dormer pawned his greatcoat and acquired a pair of pistols. Alder got hold of some powder and shot, and early in the morning, the two set out on the turnpike road from Maidenhead to Henley-on-Thames.

They hid in the bushes while Alder loaded and checked the pistols. Traffic was very light, and they waited a long time before an old man with a waggon trundled past. They decided not to attack him as he was not worth the trouble. It would be better to wait and rob a rich man than a poor one.

The two men lay in the undergrowth all morning as the watery sun climbed higher and began to wane again. There was no more traffic, and the men shivered in the wintry air, their breath coming in damp clouds, as Alder kept wiping the cheap, unreliable pistols to prevent a film of moisture forming on their flintlock mechanisms. He hoped desperately that the powder would stay dry.

The sound of horses' hooves had them reaching for their guns. The sound grew louder and nearer and they crept to the edge of the road, nerves jangling as they waited for the carriage to come into view. Their plan was that Dormer was to leap out in front, point his gun at the driver and command him to stop. Alder would then appear at the side of the coach and take whatever valuables he could get. The horses came into view, moving smartly over the frost-hard turnpike road. It was a stagecoach. Dormer drew back the hammer of his pistol to cock it ready for firing, and motioned Alder to do the same. Alder shook his head and waved his accomplice to draw close. In a hoarse whisper, he reminded his fellow robber that they had decided that stage coaches were too dangerous a target for them to tackle.

Dormer snorted his disagreement. Here was a rich prize,

ready for the taking. No-one would deny him his prey. He made to stand and make his move. His friend clamped his hand round Dormer's mouth and pulled him back into the undergrowth, the pistol a powerful reminder of Alder's superior strength and experience. A stage coach was out of the question. Dormer's enthusiasm ebbed quickly as the coach drew near. The guard sitting next to the driver was a large, grim-faced man with a three-cornered hat and a sabre scar running from his ear down to the point of his chin. In his broad leather belt was a brace of double-barrelled pistols and across his knees was a blunderbuss, a short-barrelled rifle loaded with nails and rusty lumps of metal. The guard at the rear stood with a carbine slung over his shoulder and a volley-gun on the roof of the coach. It was a seven-barrel model, designed to fire all at the same time. It was a weapon only used by men with a high degree of skill-at-arms – the recoil could knock a man off his feet. But in the right hands, it could cut a man to shreds. No-one survived a blast from a well-aimed volley-gun. Dormer and Alder were no match for these men, and they kept their heads low in the bushes as the stagecoach clattered by.

The coach passed into the distance and the two men settled down again to wait. The pale sun began to wane and Dormer's enthusiasm began to wane with it. He was on the point of trying to persuade Alder that they could go down to the ale house, The Fleece, on the Reading road close by, when the sound of horses' hooves again broke the silence. This time it was a merchant – just what the robbers were hoping for. It was an ideal target. The carriage swayed gently up the road, as the lone pedlar made his way back from Maidenhead market.

For John Robinson, it was just another day. He made a good living as a licensed hawker and pedlar in the small market towns of Berkshire and adjoining counties. He had encountered trouble with footpads before, but he was a resilient and resourceful man, and had always seen them off. Dormer jumped out of the bushes, his pistol in his hand. Shocked, Robinson stood up in his cart, just as Alder appeared at his side, pointing a pistol at his head.

The merchant was startled but he quickly recovered his composure at the sight of the two ragged robbers with their cheap flintlocks. He sneered at them and said they had better be off or they would be the worse for it. He did not seem in the least intimidated. Dormer stubbornly stood his ground, his pistol pointing at Robinson. His hand shook and Robinson struck out with his whip. It caught Alder a stinging blow across the face, and both robbers fired instinctively. The shot hit Robinson in the face. It tore a huge hole in his cheek, carried on up through the roof of his mouth and blew the top of his skull off. He slumped down at the reins of the cart and collapsed in a heap on the dusty turnpike.

The robbers looked at each other in horrified silence. Alder took a faltering step forward, Dormer looked on in dismay. Alder bent over the lifeless form and pulled at Robinson's coat. Dormer stood rooted to the spot. All the colour drained from his face as the terrible truth dawned on him. Robinson was dead. The two men looked at each other. What to do? Without even stopping to take the fat purse in Robinson's pocket, the two men ran off across the fields as fast as they could. They knew the fate that awaited them if they were caught at the scene of the crime.

Robinson's body was found by a waggoner who came past a little while later. The hue and cry went up, and the Coroner was called from Maidenhead, where the body was taken before being buried at Hurley, Robinson's home village. His family were at first distraught at his murder then angry. They wanted revenge, but the task of finding the killers in those days was exceptionally hard. This was before the days of detectives, or even a police force. Catching felons was a very difficult business.

Robinson's wife decided to offer a reward for information leading to the conviction of the murderers. Deprived of a husband who earned a very good living, and provided her with an enviable lifestyle, she was bent on retribution.

A notice appeared in the *Reading Mercury* on February 13, 1801, offering £20 reward for 'whoever will give information of the offenders, so that they may be brought to justice, shall on their conviction, receive a reward of twenty pounds of the widow of the deceased'.

It was a large amount of money - a year's wages for a poor man at the beginning of the 19th century – and tongues were soon wagging. Alder and Dormer fled to High Wycombe, but it was not far enough. Rumours of the foul deed – and the reward – were soon circulating in the taverns and ale-houses. The two had been stupid enough to boast of their venture into highway robbery, and their acquaintances' feelings of comradeship soon dwindled at the thought of the reward. Alder and Dormer were clapped in irons by the town constable and taken to Abingdon Gaol. Abingdon Gaol was a terrible place. Prison reformer John Howard inspected it in 1784, and his report said 'The straw used by the prisoners to sleep on is worn to dust, it is swarming with vermin, and there is no water for the prisoners, who are kept in irons.'

The two men were imprisoned, and interrogated, separately. Each accused the other of firing the fatal shot. It was true that both pistols had been discharged, but only one had found its mark. Dormer's hand was shaking when he aimed at the merchant, whereas Alder was cool and steadfast. The two were standing so close to each other that it was impossible to tell from which pistol the fatal shot was fired. Forensic science in those days was unheard of, and proof relied entirely on the confessions of the accused and statements of witnesses, of which there were none.

Dormer became very blasé with his inquisitors and displayed a degree of bravado which the prison officers took as an admission of guilt, although he stuck to his story that it was Alder's gun which fired the fatal shot. On the day he was to be tried for murder at Abingdon Assizes, he told a warder that he was not going to be hanged for nothing, and that if he was to be found guilty, he would murder someone before he swung from the gallows.

Alder put on a convincing performance, accusing Dormer of the murder. Dormer squirmed in the dock as Alder fired a volley of convincing lies at the jury, pretending he was merely an innocent dupe, completely in the power of the real planner and perpetrator of the crime, James Dormer.

Dormer was disgusted when Alder was acquitted and walked free, to spend that night drinking and carousing in the ale-houses of High Wycombe. The jury's decision was, in his view, a complete travesty, especially when the 12 good men and true returned from their deliberations in his own case and the judge asked them if they had reached a verdict. The foreman replied that they found James Dormer guilty of the murder of John Robinson. Dormer was a changed man when he went back to his cell. He had 48 hours to live, and spent the time collecting his thoughts, ready for the scaffold.

The death sentence changed him from a carefree, laughing young villain into a moody and foreboding one. He told prison warders he had been possessed by the devil. 'The devil has such power over me, I cannot petition the judge for mercy, I can only petition God,' he said, admitting that he was responsible for a long list of thefts and robberies. He asked for the curate of High Wycombe, Rev Williams to visit him before he died. He had lived at the rectory and worked for Mr Williams at one time, and the clergyman came immediately to counsel Dormer, a fact which brought spiritual hope to the young man.

Williams was there when Dormer was taken from the gaol to the gallows erected outside the Assize Court in the market square. It was to be a public hanging, and a large crowd of ghoulish and curious spectators gathered for the spectacle. Dormer was led in chains up the wooden steps to the gallows, where the prison chaplain prayed for his soul and sang a hymn, accompanied by Rev Williams. Silence followed, as the thousands gathered in the market square

A large crowd gathered in the market square in Abingdon to see a highwayman hanged in 1801 (photograph by Peter Bloodworth).

waited for the main part of their entertainment. Dormer
stepped forward to the wooden rail at the front of the
scaffold and raised his hand. The crowd craned forward,
sensing that Dormer was to make a speech. This was quite
rare at public hangings – most felons could just about give
their name – and a vain cry of 'I never done it!' Dormer was
different. His strict childhood education at the hands of his
conscientious family all came back to him, and he addressed
the crowd with the skill and authority of a practised orator.

'Fellow sinners,' he cried. His words rang round the square
like a peal of bells. The crowd was dumbstruck and the
silence was total. Dormer lowered his hand to the rail, the
clanking of the iron chain on his wrist clearly audible above
the heads of the crowd. 'The wretched fate you now see me
in, I brought on myself, by leading a wicked life –
particularly by sabbath-breaking, which led me on to
gambling and whoring, drinking and cock-fighting. Take
warning from me, and keep out of bad company.'

What he said next was to make the crowd gasp. 'I did not
do the deed for which I am to suffer death,' he said. Nervous
prison warders tightened their grip on his chains, and the
hangman, his face covered with a mask, shuffled his feet.
'But,' he said, his voice ringing clearly through the silence, 'I
was concerned in the act, although it was Alder who did it,
and he ought to have suffered also. This should be a warning
to judges and juries on whom they fix the crime.'

His tone changed, and the crowd shuffled and coughed
nervously as he paused, ready to continue. 'I confess,
however, that I suffer justly. Before I was sent to gaol, and
until I was condemned, I never thought of death, but, thank
God, I have now seen my mistake, and have repented in the
48 hours that were allowed me and am a very different man,
and feel myself perfectly happy. Let me appeal to all who see

what a shocking end I must come to in a few minutes. Don't go away and say 'a good fellow is gone', but repent, and turn from your evil ways – you may not know how soon death may visit you, in an hour's time, perhaps, or even less.'

His voice trailed away and he leaned on the rail to look sternly over the heads of the crowd, all come to mock him, but all now in silent captivation at his powerful words. He raised his arm, the manacles clanking as he did so, to point accusingly at the crowd. 'None of you can be sure of what may happen to you in one hour,' he said quietly. The crowd stood electrified, in total silence. 'May God change your hearts of stone into hearts of flesh,' rang out Dormer's clear voice. 'I am sorry I have acted as I have done, I have committed many offences, and though I have had many opportunities of doing well, I have neglected them all, and now it is too late. Many of you who now hear me may perhaps be intimately acquainted with my vices, and I hope those people will turn from their wicked ways and not continue in the habit of sabbath-breaking. I forgive everybody, and I hope God will forgive me the many offences I have committed.' Dormer bowed his head and stepped back to acknowledge the hangman. He asked Rev Williams to join him in singing the 121st Psalm. 'I lift up my eyes to the hills'.

The hangman put the rope around his neck, and Dormer asked if he might say a prayer before he died. His wish was granted, and he spent a few moments on his knees before stepping onto the trap with the noose around his neck, to fall to his death and avenge a pedlar, shot on the turnpike from Henley to Maidenhead.

The crowd dwindled slowly to set about its daily chores. Small groups remained to gossip, and stalls set up by enterprising traders did brisk business. Small children stared at Dormer's lifeless body as it swung from the gallows, the hangman's heavy rope creaking in the wind. Later that afternoon a group of warders from the prison came to cut down the body. Poor Dormer was not to know the final twist of terror that was to be his fate, for a stupid crime committed with little thought or planning in the cold mid-winter of 1801.

The gaolers took the body inside the courtroom, which was on the first floor of the town hall, and laid it on a trestle. The prison surgeon was ready with the grisly tools of his trade, preparing to dissect the corpse for medical research. These were the days of grave robbers, when doctors would pay huge amounts of cash for cadavers to cut up in the race for medical knowledge. Hanged murderers provided grist to the mill in a growth industry.

The surgeon cut Dormer into little pieces, his assistant making notes of the doctor's findings. As dusk fell over Abingdon market square, they put his vital organs in jars and wrapped his remains in a shroud, to be buried in an unmarked grave in the prison yard.

No-one knows what happened to Alder, the accomplice who got off scot free. Local rumour has it he was killed in a pub brawl, or was transported for another petty crime. Nothing could have been as bad as Dormer's very sticky end.

The Wife-Killer
of Warfield

IN 1851, John Carey was a smallholder who kept a pub at Warfield, near Bracknell. He was much older than his wife Hannah, and the family lived quite happily on their little farm. There was the added income from the Leathern Bottle pub, on the edge of the property run by Hannah. It was only a modest ale-house, but Hannah looked after the customers and made a modest profit.

One of the regulars was a tall young farmer called George Parker. He was a cheerful, hard-working man, handsome, attractive and good-natured. When his wife died suddenly, after a short illness, Parker was devastated. His visits to the Leathern Bottle became more frequent, where his interest in Hannah began, rapidly becoming more intense.

John Carey started to get suspicious. The family's lifestyle, with sons Alexander, aged 11 and Charles, aged 4, started to change. Hannah seemed distant. She was less and less interested in her husband and sons, and spent more and more time in the company of Parker. Her drinking increased steadily. Parker had already taken to drink after his wife died, but the two settled down to a regular pattern of consumption, with Hannah on the gin and Parker drinking ale.

This went on for nearly four years, with Carey becoming

more and more unhappy with his wife's indifference and
unfaithfulness. There was little he could do. He was by now
57 years old, and his health was failing. Parker was 35, and
powerfully built.

Carey was aware that he was going to completely lose
Hannah to Parker. The couple had been very close, and
Carey could not understand why Hannah could so easily fall
out of love with him. At one time, she had worshipped the
ground he walked on. She had loved him deeply, and he
thought, forever. He tried to grapple with the fact that she
no longer cared or wanted to be with him. It was a battle he
could not win.

In a vain attempt at appealing to her love and better
nature, he went down on his knees at her feet and implored
her to forsake Parker and return to the happy family they
had all known and loved. He only wanted to go back to how
things used to be when they were so happy.

His wife's only reply to his entreaties was to demand eight
shillings a week to keep her so that she could go to live with
Parker. John knelt on the kitchen floor and wept, his head
in his hands, the tears running down his face and onto the
cold kitchen flagstones. Hannah spurned his entreaty and
walked out of the room.

One Sunday evening in October, 1851, Carey could take
no more. He plucked up all his courage, and decided to end
his wife's relationship with his rival. Parker came into the
pub and asked for beer. Carey stood behind the counter,
cleaning tankards. He asked Parker to leave his house 'for he
had broken his peace of mind and that of his family'. Parker
stood his ground, but said nothing. Hannah stood silent
behind the bar. She took Parker's mug from the shelf and
filled it with ale. To her husband's dismay, she put it on the
counter in front of him and told her husband that while there

was beer in the house, Parker would have it.

Carey lost his temper. He picked up a wooden bucket and hurled it at Hannah with all his might. It struck her in the groin with such force that it shattered. Her eldest son, Alexander saw it all happen. Carey didn't stay to find out how much damage he had inflicted. He was terrified of Parker, and fled. The two men had once been friends, and Carey knew just how strong the farmer was.

He came home later in the evening to face his wife's taunts that he had run away from her lover. It was more than Carey could bear and he laid into her with fists and feet. His strength soon gave out, and Hannah emerged from the incident bruised and battered – but still alive. She defied him to do his worst. Taking up an axe she used for cutting firewood, she goaded him on, saying he was a feeble old man, and good for nothing except beating defenceless women. She invited him to attack her again, brandishing the axe in front of his face, and threatening to cut his head off with it.

This was to be the pattern for the next few weeks. Parker still came to the pub, but at times when he knew John Carey would be out working in his fields or tending the animals on the little farm. He would come home and regularly beat Hannah. She threatened to leave him and repeated her demand to give her money so she could go to live with Parker. This was the last straw for Carey. Again he set about her and beat her as hard as he could. He exhausted himself, leaving her with a mass of bruises, weeping pitifully in her bedroom.

Hannah took to her bed and refused to eat or drink – or to talk to her husband. Her health deteriorated fast, but Carey suspected Parker was still visiting her during the day while he was working in the fields. A few days later he came home in the evening and went upstairs, determined to settle the score with his wife. She was lying in her bed, and heard the clump of his heavy boots on the wooden stairs. She turned over to face away from him. Carey was in no fit state to talk rationally to Hannah about sorting out their failed marriage. She refused to talk to him at all, and he came quickly to the end of his tether. He told her to get up out of her bed and get out for good. She would not answer. He repeated the demand, saying this was the last time he would give her a chance to go peaceably. Hannah stayed silent.

In a fit of rage, Carey picked up her bed and ripped the mattress off the frame. With the superhuman strength of a man consumed by anger, he hurled Hannah onto the floor and threw the remains of the broken bed on top of her. Then he completely lost his senses. He picked up the bed again and threw it down on the struggling Hannah with all his might. Then he jumped on top of it, putting the whole weight of his body onto Hannah's struggling form. His nailed boots with their steel toecaps reduced the thin mattress to rags and horsehair as he jumped up and down on it. Hannah screamed as she fought to free herself from the onslaught. The couple's eight year old son, Charles, was woken by the noise and came into the room. Hannah clutched him to her breast to try and shelter from the rain of kicks and blows, but the boy's father wrenched him away and carried on.

Carey's anger guttered like a spent candle, and he collapsed, exhausted and sat back on the floor to rest. Hannah did not move. There was a slow trickle of blood coming from her mouth as she lay on the wooden boards. Carey began to panic, thinking she must be dead. He had not meant to kill her, he had merely reacted in the only way he knew how, and had lost his senses. He had loved her but she was out of his reach, and beyond his understanding. Carey was frightened. The room started to revolve around him, and he passed out.

He awoke to the cold light of dawn. It was the morning of Wednesday, October 22nd, 1851. Hannah was still stretched out on the floor where he had left her. She was still breathing although with shallow breaths, the blood dried on her face. Carey was scared and realised he should call a doctor. He mended the bed as best he could and laid Hannah in it, trying to make her as comfortable as possible. Then he ran out of the house to call Dr Walter Thompson, who lived nearby. He was the family doctor, and Carey met him in the street. He told him Hannah was sick and asked him to come straight away.

Dr Thompson found Hannah covered in bruises. He did what he could for her, and asked her if she wanted to send for someone to care for her. Hannah said she wanted her sister, Esther Bruton, who lived at Wokingham. Mrs Bruton was sent for and arrived the next day. She told the court at Carey's trial that she found her sister covered in bruises. 'She appeared very ill, she told me she had received violent kicks and blows from John, and did not believe she would recover,' said Esther. She comforted her sister as far as she could and returned home – but reported the matter to the village constable, John Wigg.

Hannah's condition worsened, and she stayed in her bed. Dr Thompson returned, this time accompanied by Mr John Westall, the surgeon from Maidenhead. They could see her condition was deteriorating, and warned her that her situation was dire.

On November 5th, two weeks after Cary inflicted the brutal beating, Hannah was to give her version of events to the local magistrate, Mr Hercy. He came to see Hannah to ask what had happened, and brought with him the Clerk to

the Justices, Mr Edward Frankum, to write down her answers
to Mr Hercy's questions. Mr Frankum said Mrs Carey was
in a 'very weak and faint state. She told the magistrate 'My
master threw the pail at me and kicked me very much. I am
in great pain, and I am certain I shall not recover.' Dr
Thompson advised Mr Hercy not to continue with the
interview because the strain would be too much for Hannah.

The next day Mrs Bruton came again from Wokingham to
see her sister. Hannah told her that she would never rise
again but would die from her husband's conduct towards
her. She asked her sister to take her after her death to
Easthampstead church to be laid by the side of her mother.
Hannah told Esther there was a bolt of calico in the
cupboard, and she wanted her to have it to make some
shirts. Esther did not want to believe her sister was going to
die, and accepted it only on condition that she should return
it when Hannah recovered.

Hannah died of her injuries on November 14th, and John
Carey was arrested next day. Constable John Wigg
accompanied him to the prison at Reading, where he was to
await trial. Carey wept bitterly and told Wigg 'I must tell you
about it. I was driven to desperation.'

John Carey appeared before Mr Justice Baron Platt at the
Berkshire Assizes on February 26th, 1852. The court heard
evidence from Dr Thompson and Mr Westall – and from
Esther Bruton, who was lusting for blood to avenge the
death of her sister. She is reported to have said that she
would go 50 miles to see John Carey hang.

Dr Thompson told the court he had conducted a post
mortem examination of Mrs Carey. 'The injuries were
severe,' he said. 'I found the marks of bruises on the lower
part of the back, between the shoulders, and on the legs and
insteps. Internally there was evidence of inflammation on the

abdomen, on one side a large abscess had formed, caused by the external bruising. The inflammation was sufficient to cause her death.' He declared she must have led a temperate life, but admitted she had liver and kidney infection which indicated she may have recently taken to drink.

Mr Westall, the surgeon who assisted Dr Thompson at the post mortem, said 'I have never before seen such intense suffering to the abdomen.' Esther Bruton was called to the witness stand. 'John Carey came home in the evening and started to abuse my sister,' she told the court. 'He went upstairs into her bedroom and was going to strike her. She took her child and laid it across her breast to prevent him striking her. Then he pulled the child out of the way and pulled her out of bed onto the floor and commenced striking and kicking her in the side and in the groin, and on different parts of her person. Then he pulled the bed off the bedstead and put it upon her, and threw himself down upon it, and jumped upon it. She crawled from under the bed on her hands and knees and into an adjoining room to try and escape further ill-treatment. He followed her to the other room and was kicking her feet and legs, which caused a great many bruises, and the skin and flesh were torn by his tipped and nailed boots. The violence was so bad that one of her toenails was completely torn away from her right foot. She was dreadfully bruised. Carey left her to suffer. He said she would not die yet – she had not been punished enough.'

Carey's 15 year old son Alexander was called to the stand. 'Did your mother drink much?' asked the judge. 'Yes, often,' replied the boy. 'She used to drink gin, and I have often been obliged to take the gin away from her when she got drunk. She sometimes got drunk with Parker. I remember my father going down upon his hands and knees, entreating her not to drink or go with Parker. We lived happily until two years

ago, the quarrelling did not commence until Parker came to
the house. He came frequently to my father's. He was there
every day till she took to her bed. He would come after my
father had gone out, and went before he returned. My
mother and father quarrelled very often on account of
Parker.'

Constable John Wigg took the stand. 'I have known
Parker 20 years,' he told the court. 'He is aged about 35, and
is a very athletic and powerful man. For strength and
activity, he was as much more powerful than Carey as the
horse is the hen. The Careys lived happily until Parker's wife
died about four years ago.'

The barrister conducting Carey's defence, Mr John
McMahon, addressed the jury. He reminded them that
Carey had gone to fetch the doctor for his wife, and had even
gone to the trouble to fetch the surgeon, Mr Westall, from
Maidenhead. He threw doubt on the medical evidence which
showed Mrs Carey had died from her bruises, and
emphasised that the post mortem had shown she had been
drinking for some time. Then he turned his attention to the
evidence given by Hannah Carey's sister.

'This case is exceedingly aggravated by the evidence of the
deceased's sister, Mrs Bruton,' he said. 'Her conduct has
throughout been somewhat remarkable. You will remember
she said in her evidence that she would go 50 miles to see
Carey hanged; therefore it is not for the gentlemen of the jury
to be too impressed with the statements of Mrs Bruton. I beg
also to draw to your attention that when Carey refused
Parker beer, the deceased declared that while there was beer
in the house, Parker should have it.

'Can you be surprised that a man could witness the
violation of his domestic relationship, can you not be
surprised that when the law would not visit with its

vengeance the murder of a party who was guilty of such
infidelity, but would designate it justifiable homicide, that a
poor man, goaded by the treachery of his wife, should – on
the spur of the moment, and in the heat of blood – commit
an act such as that for which the prisoner at the bar stands
arraigned before you. I am convinced that after taking all the
facts into consideration, you will decide in favour of the
prisoner.'

Mr Justice Baron Platt summed up the case. 'As regards
the deceased's wife having said that if he would give her eight
shillings a week she would leave him and go to Parker, the
law protects every man against having to pay the support of
his wife when she commits adultery, for then she becomes an
outcast, and lost altogether to society. It is now, gentlemen,
for you to say whether the evidence produced is such as to
convict the prisoner of killing his wife. However much he
might not intend it, if he did so he renders himself
responsible for the act.'

The jury found Carey guilty, but made a strong
recommendation of mercy. The judge told him 'John Carey,
yours is a very dreadful case. It is true that your wife was
guilty of gross misconduct, such as was, no doubt, calculated
to excite and exasperate you. But at the same time, if the
injuries had been inflicted in the moment of your wrath and
not in your cool moments, then the court might have dealt
more leniently with you. But, you came home one night and
without any cause of aggravation, caused the death of this
poor, unhappy, guilty creature. You came home, ferociously
dragged her out of bed and trampled on her. There is no
doubt that the injuries received were the cause of her death.
This is really very shocking.'

Mr Justice Baron Platt paused to let the words sink in. 'It
is impossible to visit you with a light sentence. I had a notion

that I should transport you for the greater portion of your life. It is quite impossible that you can be allowed to remain in this country. If such barbarous conduct were passed over with a light punishment, we do not know what effect it might have upon others, in deterring them from committing mischief and cruelty. The sentence of this court is that you be transported for seven years.

Carey broke down in the dock and cried bitterly. 'I beg you my lord, do not send me out of the country,' he pleaded.

'What did the old man say?' asked the judge. He told Carey he felt for the two children, Alexander and Charles, who would now be orphans, but there was no alternative to the sentence. 'I have thought this matter over carefully, and I find it is impossible I can pass over this,' he told Carey. 'Take the prisoner down.'

THE MADMAN
AND THE PIGLET

JOHN and Elizabeth Cannon and their family lived a respectable and uneventful life at Boyn Hill in the Borough of Maidenhead. But terrible consequences were to follow the arrival of Elizabeth's brother Isaac in 1852 for an indefinite stay.

Isaac Lee had been a successful brushmaker in London. His business did well, and he became prosperous. But his world had collapsed around him when his wife died. The elderly couple had been close all their lives and the loss of his beloved wife had driven him to the edge of insanity.

Isaac ended up in the hospital of St Mary of Bethlehem in London. It was known colloquially as Bedlam – a word which has come into the English language to signify any mad scene, and the horrors of the place were well illustrated by the satirical cartoonists of the time. Life in Bedlam was more than Isaac could stand. So Isaac wrote to John Cannon, his sister's husband and offered him considerable financial reward if he could go and live with them. John Cannon and his wife considered the prospect long and hard. They were not greedy people, but they knew Isaac had money salted away and that he would be quite generous if he was allowed to come and live with them. He had no other family and the

Cannons were Isaac's only lifeline. But they knew what he was like, with his blackouts and periods of strange behaviour. The combination of financial inducement of £50 per year – a handsome figure in those days – coupled with their genuine concern for Isaac's welfare, decided them to let him come and live with them – a decision they were to rue for the rest of their lives.

Isaac lived with them for about two years. Sometimes he was troublesome, sometimes he was not. His sister kept a close eye on him all of the time – and locked the knives away in the kitchen. Isaac kept his promise to pay his way. One morning in March, 1852, Mrs Cannon was called urgently by a neighbour. After making sure her brother was all right, she left him on his own. Isaac wandered off outside the cottage, and then went back indoors. His four year old great-niece Lizzie, John Cannon's grand-daughter, was in the kitchen. She had been staying at the house, even though her parents, James and Eliza Cannon, lived close by. Isaac sat down in his chair. It was early morning, and a small piglet came in from the yard in the hope of finding some scraps on the kitchen floor.

Isaac saw red. For some reason the presence of the tiny piglet turned him from being a mild-mannered old man into a raging monster. He picked up a billhook, a heavy curved blade used for trimming hedges, and stalked the piglet across the kitchen. He raised his arm with the hook, and it came crashing down on the piglet's head. The animal squealed violently as it crashed to the floor, covered in blood. The blow was so violent it broke both the pig's jaws as it brought it down. Isaac's hand was raised again. The pig lurched to its feet and crawled under a shelf in the scullery in a flurry of blood and squeals. The heavy hook missed its mark, and skidded across the flagstones in a shower of sparks. Isaac bent to retrieve it, and stood by the door with the bloodstained hook in his hand.

Little Lizzie Cannon screamed in terror. She took one look at wild-eyed Isaac and tried to run past him to the kitchen door. He stepped back and blocked her way. He did not want to let her leave the kitchen – he did not know why. He lashed out, still holding the vicious hook – until Lizzie's screams grew quiet.

The noise attracted curious neighbours, who were quickly on the scene and appalled at what they found. Messages were sent to call John and Elizabeth Cannon, the child's mother, Eliza, and the constable, Simeon Frewin. Lizzie's

Maidenhead Police Station in the mid 19th century.

body was taken outside and placed on a board. Isaac, who seemed to have calmed down immediately after the incident, became noisy and excitable. As the constable approached, he became violent and tried to escape.

'It took four of us to put the handcuffs on him, it was a job to hold him down,' Constable Frewin told the inquest jury. 'The deceased was lying on a table, quite dead, and the head and face were a gore of blood. I found an old hook with some blood on it, and a small dead pig, about a fortnight old. I and four others removed Isaac Lee to the Union. His trousers and shoes were covered in blood, and so was the floor.' The Union was the workhouse, which also doubled as a lock-up for the constable. Isaac Lee was taken from there to the prison at Reading to await the outcome of the inquest and the hearing in the magistrates court.

Several witnesses described how they arrived to find Isaac in a daze. 'He was as white as a sheet,' said one. The coroner's jury, after hearing of Lizzie's horrific injuries – of which Isaac could remember nothing – recorded a verdict of 'wilful murder' against him, but he was found unfit to plead. He spent the rest of his days back in Bedlam, the madhouse he had made such an effort – and spent so much money – to escape from.

THE LAST
PUBLIC HANGING

THE Borough police force at Windsor knew John Gould as a violent, ill-tempered lout who would fly off the handle at the slightest provocation. He would lash out with fists and feet in a blind rage, especially when he was drunk – which was often. He was a big, mean man, powerfully built, and earned his living as a bricklayer's labourer. He had come to blows on numerous occasions with the police, some of whom had received a beating for their pains. Gould was 39 years old, and had already served three terms of imprisonment for his violent behaviour. It was just after Christmas in 1861, and Gould was in holiday mood. For him, that meant not going to work for the week, and devoting his time to some serious drinking.

On December 30th, he spent the morning in the Prince of Wales, his local pub in Clewer village. He staggered home in the afternoon to find the only person at the small house at Clarence Clump was his seven year old daughter, Hannah.

It was cold, and Hannah was busy lighting the fire in the parlour to try and keep herself warm. She cleaned out the ashes in a bucket, and put paper and sticks in the grate. There was coal at the side of the hearth for when the flames were strong enough. Hannah put a piece of newspaper over the fireplace to let the draught turn the smoking heap into a blaze that would keep her warm.

Her father stumbled into the room and rounded on her in a drunken rage. Red-eyed and spoiling for a fight, he told her the house was in a disgusting mess and it was her job to clean it up. She was frightened and backed away from him, shaking her head. He took his razor from the shelf and – with not a word of warning – cut her throat. Hannah's body slid slowly from his grasp, and with barely a whimper, she was dead on the bare floorboards, the red blood oozing from the gash in her neck. Gould panicked. He went out into the street. He saw a neighbour, Mrs Sarah Clark. He stuttered to her that he had just killed Hannah. Mrs Clark did not know what to do. She stepped back from Gould as she realised the awful truth, that Gould was not just a violent drunk, he was a murdering drunk. Her backward steps quickened as she screamed and ran for help.

Gould's fuddled brain could only muster one reaction – anger. He became extremely agitated, and went back into the house. He picked up the child's blood-soaked body and threw it forcibly out of the door. The little corpse landed like a rag doll at the foot of the wall outside. The police arrived in force. They knew Gould's reputation, and he lived up to it by putting up a fierce struggle in an attempt to escape. He was overpowered and taken into custody, to be charged with the wilful murder of his daughter.

Windsor magistrates sent him to await trial at Reading Assizes, where he was tried and found guilty. His only defence against the charge was that he was drunk. He was sentenced to be hanged publicly.

Whilst awaiting trial, and subsequent execution, Gould was imprisoned at Reading Gaol, which had been built to the 'new model prison' design and was opened in 1844. It was of 'radial' design, similar to Pentonville prison in London, on the site of a smaller gaol and house of correction built in 1795. The new prison cost the taxpayers £44,000.

There was considerable opposition among the wealthier classes to the death penalty and a number of people tried hard to save Gould from the gallows. Well-wishers made several last-ditch attempts to get him reprieved, with over 400 people signing a petition to the Home Secretary. Their efforts came to nothing, except to postpone the fateful day of execution, which was set for noon on March 14th, 1862. It was to be carried out by the public executioner, William Calcraft, who was Britain's longest serving – and probably most incompetent – hangman. Calcraft was born near Chelmsford in 1800 and was apprenticed as a boot and shoe maker. He was drawn to the big city, and became a pieman, selling his wares to the crowds gathered round the gallows at Newgate. He got to know the hangmen there, and got into their grisly trade by offering himself as an assistant. The prison governor decided to give him a try. He considered Calcraft a quiet, sober, respectable citizen, who lived with his wife and two sons – and kept pet rabbits. He was appointed executioner for London and Middlesex in April, 1829, at a weekly wage of one guinea, plus a bonus of a guinea for every hanging. Although Calcraft did not retire until he was 70, he never acquired the required degree of competence in his job. Most of his victims died of slow strangulation, instead of the quick, neck-breaking death they were supposed to suffer. He always gave his victims a short drop and tied the noose – of thick, coarse rope – in a clumsy knot. It was common to see his assistant climb under the gallows to pull the victim's legs to hasten death.

Calcraft had become brutalised by his work and was by now a deeply unpopular figure. He wore dirty black clothes and a tall black hat. His face was craggy and his voice was

Windsor Borough Constabulary, 1904.

low and sinister. He was accustomed to being disliked – but people always turned up in their thousands to watch him at work. He was used to performing before crowds of up to 100,000. No figures are available for Gould's hanging, but it is not likely the crowd was that large.

On the Monday before the execution, Gould was visited at the prison by his sister. She was very shaken by the experience, and as soon as she entered his cell, she fainted.

She recovered, and visited again next day, along with Gould's wife and other daughter. The parting between husband and wife was very touching and tearful. She had forgiven him all his past sins. 'The couple prayed together in sorrow and tears,' reported the local paper. 'He had always resigned himself to his fate, and he prayed most of the night before his death, being joined by the chaplain, Rev J B

Colville, in the morning.'

When the Under-Sheriff and the Governor came for him shortly before noon, he said to the chaplain 'May the Lord bless you, and give you many blessings for all you have done for me. Give my love to my family and tell them I remembered them.'

The crowd of thousands came from miles around, and special trains were laid on for the occasion. The mob was so huge it stretched from the prison gate as far back as the railway line and beyond. Special areas were cordoned off for the county's nobles and notables, and everyone jostled to get a better view. Despite it being a cold morning, many arrived early to get the best spot to view the grisly scene.

The Berkshire Chronicle recorded that the crowd consisted of people from every level of society. 'There were the young and the old, the rich and the poor, those who belonged to the better class of society and those whose attire denoted abject poverty. There were mothers with little children in their arms, there was lusty youth and hoary age. There was an extraordinarily high proportion of women. Their presence on such an occasion was all the more to be wondered at when it is recollected that an execution is not only revolting to the sight, but it is a trying ordeal to the strongest nerves. However, they seemed to take a sort of exultant interest in the spectacle, which did but little honour to their taste, their good feeling or their humanity.'

Gould walked to the gallows with his Bible in his hand, and looked with a steady and unflinching eye upon the multitude below. The scaffold had been erected on the gatehouse tower in Forbury Road, and the crowd stretched back beyond the railway line. 'There was no sign of fear in his countenance or his gait', said the *Chronicle* reporter. It took less than five minutes for Calcraft to get him ready to open the trap. Gould's face was covered, his legs strapped with leather straps, and the noose adjusted around his neck. He handed his Bible to the chaplain for it to be returned to his family. The drop fell, there was a slight convulsion, and the soul of the poor man was launched into eternity, with the last words 'May God have mercy upon my soul.' After the customary one hour, Gould's body was taken down and buried in the prison yard.

The editor of the *Berkshire Chronicle* felt sufficiently moved to run a very long comment in the paper next day. 'This unhappy being expiated his crime at noon yesterday. It is many years since an execution has been held in this town, the last being in 1846. The full atrocity of his deed was revealed in the Assize Court, where it was proved how a poor, helpless and unoffending girl fell victim to the wanton barbarity of its parent. His life was one of profligacy and unchecked violence. He followed the occupation of bricklayer's labourer, and with his stalwart frame and not unintelligent mind, he might have earned a good livelihood. But he was given to vicious habits, to idleness and drunkenness. His violent behaviour had led to him being imprisoned on three occasions prior to this matter. Twice he was confined at Reading and once at Aylesbury Gaol. These punishments appear to have had no salutory effect on him. He still continued in his bad ways, and his wife and child still had to submit to his brutality. His fellow workmen were also the subject of his violence, until he became a terror to the neighbourhood. To the police he was well-known as about the most lawless character to be found in the town of Windsor.'

It was almost as if Gould was born to die on the gallows. And he achieved the dubious distinction of being the last man to be publicly hanged in the county.

Revenge is Sweet?

IN 1866 at a cottage in Smith's Crescent, Newbury, Henry Martin was living with a woman called Eliza Shaw, a prostitute on whose earnings Martin lived. He had been sacked from his job as a butcher's assistant for cheating a serving-girl out of a large sum of money. He was a powerfully-built man, but showed no inclination to work. He was quite happy to live off Eliza – as long as he remained her master.

Martin had been sentenced to a month in Reading Gaol for trying to rob a man at Thatcham. He had almost garotted the man, a Mr Messenger, in order to steal his purse. Martin was caught and sent to prison.

Henry Martin was not happy in prison. He had heard the woman he lived with had been seen about the town with another man. He counted the days to his release and plotted terrible revenge.

Eliza came from a family of travelling barge people, who plied their trade regularly up and down the Kennet and Avon Canal. She had grown up in Newbury and had also lived in Union Street, Reading, known locally as 'smelly alley'. The local paper described it at the time as 'one of the most disreputable parts of the town'. Union Street – and the tenement buildings opposite, where the Sainsbury's supermarket and shopping mall now stand – were hotbeds of petty crime and violence then.

Eliza had come back to Newbury to ply her dubious trade and had fallen under Martin's evil influence. He was cruel and brutally violent, and it came as a relief to her when he was sent to gaol. She took up with the barman at the Eagle public house in Bartholomew Street. He came from London, and his name was James Brett. Eliza pitched her cap at him as a replacement to the brutal Martin, who she knew would come looking for her when he got out of prison.

She was right. Martin heard about Brett, and realised he would lose his income if Eliza ditched him. He came out of prison at the end of November, 1866, and headed for the Eagle for a showdown. The only thing on his mind was to settle the score – to get rid of James Brett, and reclaim Eliza Shaw, his meal ticket. Eliza had sent messages that he was not to come near, or she would sell all her possessions and run off with Brett. Martin was not impressed. He walked into the ale-house to confront the couple, with murder in his mind.

Witnesses later described the ugly scene to the coroner at the inquest. William Wyatt – whose father was the policemen on patrol outside – said he was in the Eagle when Martin came in to warn Brett off, and try to reclaim what he saw as his property – Elizabeth Shaw. An abusive quarrel developed.

'Jimmy and Eliza were both very drunk,' Mr Wyatt told the coroner. 'Martin called her a lot of filthy names, and she hit him. She slapped his face and grabbed him by the hair, pulled him out of his seat and threw him on the floor.' Martin, knowing that policemen were outside in the street, did not immediately retaliate.

Brett and Eliza decided to leave and go to her cottage for the night. The landlady saw trouble brewing and closed the doors, ordering everyone to leave. It was past midnight –

there were no licensing laws in those days – and the customers drifted out. Wyatt and Martin were among the last to go.

'Martin asked me to get a hammer or a pickaxe for him,' said Wyatt. 'I did not do so because I thought he would go and give Jimmy and Eliza a good hiding.'

Wyatt tried to persuade Martin to come and stay the night with him, but Martin was bent on mischief. 'Revenge is sweet,' he told Wyatt. 'But I will not swing for them.'

The two men wandered down the street and stood talking in the pig market – now the Kennet Centre car park. 'Martin asked me to go to Shaw's house with him,' Wyatt told the inquest. 'He was not drunk – but seemed to be confused and trying to work things out. I told him to come home with me, but he stood up, shook me by the hand and said "Good night, Bill, God bless you. Revenge is sweet." He walked away, and I never saw him again.'

Martin walked through the inky-black streets to Shaw's cottage at Eyles's Buildings, in what is now known as Shaw Road. No-one saw him as he used his butcher's cramp – a steel rod with a hook at one end and a hammer at the other – to prise open the shutters.

He crept up the wooden staircase to find Jimmy and Eliza naked and asleep in bed. He hesitated in the darkness. It was cold, and he shivered at the thought of the terrible deed he had come to do. He grabbed Brett by the hair and pulled his head back, slashing him across the throat with a knife. It did not kill him straight away, but the disturbance woke Eliza. Martin set about her with his butcher's hook. She screamed as he rained blows down on her head, fracturing her skull. She put her hands up to try and save her face, but he broke her knuckles with the hammer. Then he ripped into her with the hook. He broke off to smash Brett's skull with the hammer, then turned back to Eliza. He left the couple in a pool of blood and escaped out of the window.

The neighbours had been awoken by Eliza's screams, but thought nothing of it. Violent rows had been common in the Martin household. The neighbours went back to sleep, blissfully unaware of the deed of blood in their midst.

As dawn broke, they woke to sleepily wonder what had happened during the night. Eliza's neighbours gathered outside in Eyles's Yard. Mrs Emily Banning drew her shawl tightly round her and asked widow Charlotte Goddard if she too had heard the row in Martin's house. Although both women were reluctant to interfere in their neighbours' business, they decided they should investigate. The two women crept gingerly into the cottage. Mrs Goddard went to the foot of the staircase. Upstairs, Eliza was dead, and Jimmy Brett was dying. Widow Goddard heard his noisy breathing as his life ebbed away in a trickle of blood. Mrs Goddard did not know there was a man in the house, and assumed it was Eliza Shaw. Relieved to think she was all right, they departed about their own business.

Martin went to his mother's house, woke her up, wished her farewell, and left. He went looking for the man Messenger, whom he had tried to rob, for which crime he had been sent to prison. But his search for his third victim of terrible revenge was unsuccessful. Amazingly, he decided to return to the scene of his crime. The *Berkshire Chronicle* reported 'At about eight o'clock, Martin, who seems to have been a man of iron nerve, returned to the house where he knew his victims to be. The spot where the crimes were committed seems to have a strange fascination for murderers, and perhaps in no other way can we account for this man's re-visit to the scene of his infamy. The murderer also made enquiries as to whether any disturbance had been

Eyles's Buildings, Newbury was the scene of an horrific murder in 1862 (photograph by Peter Bloodworth).

heard in the night. That he was a desperate man, and in a mood desperate enough for any atrocity, there can be no question'.

Martin then walked off into town, and headed for the Crown public house at West Mills. Mrs Goddard went again to the cottage. This time she went upstairs to find the scene of terrible carnage. She ran out of the house and raised the alarm. A boy was sent to run for the police.

By nine o'clock Superintendent Harfield had arrived from Newbury police station. A doctor arrived in a vain attempt to save Brett, who died of his injuries a short while later. The superintendent described the scene to the coroner's court.

'In a room upstairs I found Eliza Shaw, whom I knew perfectly well. She was quite dead, and enveloped with blood. I also saw a man on the floor who was dying from severe wounds. It was James Brett. I left the man under medical care and from information received, I concluded that Henry Martin was the murderer, and I went in search of him.'

Mrs Banning's young daughter Tryphena told the court 'We live next door to Mrs Martin. About a quarter to two o'clock I heard her call out 'Murder! murder! Lord save me!' I heard Martin say 'If you holloa again, I will do for you.' Then there was a thud, like someone falling on the floor.'

Dr Silas Palmer, the Speenhamland physician, told the coroner how he was called to the scene. 'I saw Eliza Shaw lying on the bed, quite dead,' he said. 'There was a wound over her right brow, three to four inches in length, penetrating to the brain. The skull was fractured and the brain exposed. The top of the head was driven in, and the brain scattered over her. The pillow and bed were saturated with blood. She was dead, and these wounds caused her death. The man was in a state of stupor from the wounds he had received. He had as many as 10 wounds on his face and head. I removed from the skull a portion of the bone, which I now produce in court. The man died at about one o'clock.

The jury took only five minutes to return a verdict of wilful murder against Henry Martin, as Martin knew they were bound to do. He knew he would be the prime suspect, and he knew the penalty. The last public hanging in the County had been in 1862, but that was of no comfort to Martin. To be hanged, even in the privacy of the cold prison yard at Reading Gaol was not a prospect to look forward to.

Superintendent Harfield did not take long to find witnesses who had seen Martin heading for the Crown Inn at West Mills, on the south bank of the Kennet and Avon Canal. Martin had drunk a glass of ale there and chatted with other customers before setting off up the towpath

Northbrook Street, Newbury as it looked when murder victim Eliza Shaw plied her dubious trade in 1866 (reproduced by kind permission of Mr Lewis of Headley).

towards the footbridge at Northcroft. There, he calmly sat down on the bank and took off his hat and boots. It was a cold, quiet day, and there was no-one around as he took a neck-scarf from his pocket and tied it round his ankles. Then he jumped into the freezing brown water. His farewell to his mother was complete.

Superintendent Harfield had arrived at the Crown to be told Martin had walked off up the river bank. A man came running towards him to say there was a body floating downstream. It was Henry Martin.

Harfield ordered the body to be pulled out of the water and taken to a nearby stable, belonging to a Mr Nias, founder of a Newbury garage. Harfield found Martin's cap and boots on the towpath where he had left them. There was no doubt whatsoever that it was the body of Henry Martin. The killer was caught, but never to see the hangman's noose. As he had promised William Wyatt on the night he planned the dreadful deed of blood, standing in the cold night air at Newbury pig market, he would never swing for it!

DEATH AT THE
CROSSROADS

INSPECTOR Drewett and Constable Shorter were patrolling the Folly Crossroads area north of Hungerford in search of poachers one cold December night in 1876. PC Golby had just started his night duty at 10 pm and was waiting for Inspector Drewett to rendezvous with him in the dimly lit High Street. He was not too concerned then.

It was not unusual for officers to be late. Hungerford police station covered a vast rural area where poaching and poverty went hand in hand. Policemen in those days had no cars or personal radios. They patrolled on foot, and passed on information at pre-arranged meeting-places, or 'conference points'. PC Golby knew that Inspector Drewett was due to meet PC Shorter at the crossroads and set off to find him. He walked in darkness past Eddington church – now a private house – and carried on up the hill. Suddenly he saw a figure lying in the road. He thought it was a drunk and went to investigate. He was wrong. To his horror, it was his colleague, PC Thomas Shorter. He had been battered to death. His face was so badly bruised and beaten he was almost unrecognisable.

His heart pounding, PC Golby ran back to the gatehouse at the beginning of the turnpike. He roused the gatekeeper, William Hedges, and ordered the old man and his terrified

PC Shorter and Inspector Drewett (on facing page) were brutally killed by poachers in 1876.

wife to keep watch in case anyone went past. Then PC Golby went for help. He made it back to the police station and blurted out his incredible story. He did not know it, but worse was to come. A message was despatched to Newbury to summon Superintendent George Bennett with all speed. Arrangements were made for PC Shorter's body to be examined and removed from the scene of the crime.

Golby started back up the hill to search for Inspector Drewett, accompanied by PC Charles Brown from Kintbury.

By now, it was well into the small hours of the morning and the two officers walked in total darkness back to the scene of horror.

They reached Folly Crossroads and split up. Golby took the left hand lane to Chilton Foliat, and Brown turned right to Denford.

Within minutes, PC Brown had found Inspector Drewett's battered body lying on the grass verge. He had been shot through the neck at point blank range, and his head had been smashed like an eggshell. His truncheon had not been drawn and there was no sign of a struggle having taken place –

exactly the same circumstances as PC Shorter's death.

Help was now arriving from Newbury. Superintendent Bennett had rushed by pony and trap with extra men, and a full-scale search was started. Within an hour, he learned that two men had passed through the turnpike gate and had been seen by William Hedges, the gatekeeper. Their names were William Day, a 39 year old labourer, and William Tidbury, aged 24, Day's son-in-law. Both men lived in a row of cottages at Eddington and worked at Cottrell's iron foundry. Day was suspected by police of being the leader of a gang of poachers.

Soon after 7 am, Superintendent Bennett arrived at Day's cottage to arrest him. Day was just finishing his breakfast. He was charged and taken to Hungerford police station. Soon after, he was joined in the cells by William Tidbury and his brothers Henry, aged 26, and Francis, aged 17. All four were under lock and key by 9 am.

West Berkshire was shocked at the violent double murder. The next issue of the local paper said 'Little did the inhabitants dream as they were fastening their doors and preparing for bed on the night in question that a tragedy of horrors was being enacted within a mile of the town hall, which should surpass in atrocity anything known in the neighbourhood within the memory of those living and would create a shudder in many some miles away.'

The coroner held the inquest at the John O'Gaunt Inn in Hungerford. The two bodies were laid out in the straw in the coach house in the same condition in which they had been found. The newspaper report said 'The spectacle was one that touched the hearts of all, and strong men looked as if they could readily weep at the sight of the powerful men who had been the victims of such diabolical treatment.'

Hungerford went into full mourning for the funeral of the

two murdered policemen. They were buried in Eddington churchyard – just a stone's throw away from the spot where they were so brutally murdered.

The four prisoners were committed for trial at Reading Assizes, before Mr Justice Lindley. Crowds besieged the court, and had to be controlled by police. Admission to the hearing was by ticket only, and spaces in court were reserved for the county gentry.

The four accused pleaded not guilty. Huge crowds surrounded the court as the evidence unfolded. Dr Harry Major, Hungerford's local doctor, told the court Inspector Drewett had 40 shotgun pellets in a neck wound, but had died of severe brain injuries. Every bone was broken in PC Shorter's head – both men had been battered to death.

In his summing up, Mr Justice Lindley said most of the evidence was mainly circumstantial. The jury retired and all eyes rested on the four men whose lives were in the balance.

Two hours later, the foreman announced the verdict. William Day and William Tidbury were not guilty. Henry and Francis Tidbury were guilty. The judge put on his black cap and passed sentence of death on the two men. His lordship praised the police for their 'creditable diligence'. PC Golby was promoted to the rank of sergeant.

The sentence caused widespread controversy in Berkshire. Many people were astonished that Day and William Tidbury escaped the noose. On the other hand, Francis Tidbury was only 17 years old. A mercy plea to the Home Secretary failed, and the two brothers were led to the gallows on the morning of March 12, 1877.

The black flag fluttered over the prison until the bodies were cut down. Public hanging had recently been abolished and the executions took place in the photographing room, witnessed by press reporters who were given copies of the

BRUTAL MURDER!!
In Berkshire.

On Monday, December 11th, Inspector Drewitt, and P. C. Shorter were found murdered on the high road, one mile from Hungerford. Four desperate Poachers are in custody for the crime.

Tune—Driven from Home.

A barbarous murder on the country road side,
All throughout Berkshire is spread far and wide ;
An Inspector of police, and a private as well,
Both have been murdered, we're sorry to tell.
Upon Monday night their bodies were found
By another Policeman on his lonely round ;
When near Dewford toll-bar a sight met his gaze,
He'll never forget to the end of his days.

CHORUS.

Near Hungerford, in Berkshire, on a lonely road
    side,
Two Policemen by a murder so cruel they died ;
Quite dead and cold they were both of them found,
Their brains beaten out as they lay on the ground.

A more unmanly crime has seldom been known,
I am sure you will say if your hearts are not stone,
To take poor men's lives in cold blood we must say,
Is not like an Englishman's love of fair play ;
They must have been beaten to death on the ground,
Till the blood of the victims in pools lay around !
They gave them no chance their lives to defend,
The unequall struggle soon came to an end.

The eleventh of December, a dark gloomy night,
The two men were found, what a sad ghastly sight !
By the police of the district the alarm was soon
    spread,
Much sympathy was shown for the poor murdered
    dead.
Four men were taken with blood on their clothes,
Whether they are guilty God only knows !
We will not condemn, tho' they bear a bad name,
If they are the murderers so much to their shame.

Two of the men who are taken, they say,
Must have passed down the road where the two
    bodies lay ;
The man at the toll gate saw them go through.
He watch'd for their coming as he'd been told to do ;
They seem'd agitated and hurried along,
Suspicion against them has been very strong ;
Let us take care that none but the guilty shall fall,
Tho' this world's full of trouble, life's dear to us all.

Four men are charged with this cruel crime,
The charge they must answer at the proper time ;
Two men have been killed, and justice will say,
The murderers we know cannot be far away.
Blood for blood has long been the law of the land,
And in crimes that are done with a cowardly hand,
It is nothing but right such men should be taught
The revenge of a murderer is too dearly bought.

These Policemen, no doubt, have left children and
    wives,
Who are plunged in a sorrow that will last them
    their lives ;
They will never forget where'er they may roam,
The night when they brought these poor murdered
    men home.
Their prospects in future are blighted and gone,
We hope they're not friendless altho' they're alone,
As they stand by the grave of those they love best,
May their prayers be heard for the dear ones at rest.

London :—H. P. SUCH, Machine Printer and
Publisher, 177, Union-street, Borough.

confessions the two men gave before being taken to the gallows.

Two memorial crosses were erected by the roadside near where the two policemen fell. They were restored some years ago, and still stand in silent tribute to two brave men who died in the course of their duty.

When they were so brutally killed Drewett was 42 years old. He was a native of Weston, near Welford, and was married with five children. Shorter, aged 24, was a married man who came from Bray, near Maidenhead. A public subscription raised a large sum for the two widows.

THE WARREN
FARM TRAGEDY

WHEN Superintendent George Bennett arrived at Warren Farm near Newbury on a freezing cold night in January, 1891, he found two people dead and another out of his mind with grief. Superintendent Bennett was a veteran of gory murder scenes, but even he was appalled at what he found. He described the scene as 'the most horrible' he had ever witnessed.

Warren Farm is just off the Andover Road at Wash Common, a leafy, pleasant suburb on the south side of Newbury. The house was occupied by Mr John Chamberlain and his wife Annie Maria, who came from a well-known and much respected local family called Heath.

The Heath family were farmers and lived at Boames Farm, Enborne. George Heath was a typical countryman, honest and upright, but now getting on in years. His son, Sydney, aged 31, was married and lived with his wife and three children in a new house on the road from Newbury to Wash Common. His daughter, Annie Maria, had been married to Mr John Chamberlain for the past 15 months, and the couple lived close by at Warren Farm.

The Chamberlains were very happy, lived a comfortable existence, and were regular worshippers at the nearby Methodist chapel, where Sydney Heath was the organist. He was a talented player, and much in demand at church gatherings to play hymns and songs. His sister and brother-in-law were also prominent members of the church.

The family was very close, and in times of trouble stood by one another readily. Thus it was that Sydney answered his sister's call when she told him she wanted to discuss some family business.

It was early evening when Sydney met the Wash Common postman, Snook, at his front gate. He wished him good evening and strolled up the road to Warren Farm to see his sister and brother-in-law, John Chamberlain. John had just made his will, and the three were to discuss some of the minor details.

All seemed well as they talked in the small sitting room. John had appointed Annie and Sydney joint executors of his will. He was comfortably off and the will was a matter for serious consideration. Annie told her husband she wanted to talk to her brother privately for a few moments, and asked John if he would mind leaving them. Sydney was seated at the piano, playing a short piece of music to amuse himself. Suspecting nothing, John readily agreed and closed the door behind him. He walked across the hall and into the kitchen, his thoughts on the finer legal points of the will he had just signed. There was the dull hum of conversation for a few minutes, and he heard Sydney start to play the piano. He played beautifully, the cheerful notes of his sister's favourite melody. Annie loved to hear her brother play, it soothed and comforted her.

In the kitchen, John smiled to himself. Humming along with the tune, his thoughts returned to the niceties of the legal documents – until he heard the gunshot.

The piano music became a crashing discord, then silence. John stood rooted to the spot for what seemed an eternity.

The gun was deafening – and so close. His legs seemed like jelly as he forced himself to run the few short paces to the sitting room. He flung open the door and took in the awful sight before him. His wife Annie stood in the middle of the room, a smoking shotgun in her hand. The report of the *Newbury Weekly News* at the time describes the scene. 'She had crept up softly behind her brother and literally blown his brains out. Death, happily, must have been instantaneous, as the left side of the skull was completely blown off into a corner of the room, while the poor fellow's brains bespattered the piano, the sheet of music, the furniture, and the wall.'

Sydney's body was slumped over the keyboard, the oozing red blood a stark contrast with the black and white notes. Horrified, John turned to his wife. There was another cartridge in the breech and she had her finger on the trigger. John lunged at her to try and take the gun, but she clung on tightly and would not let go. The couple struggled, Annie trying to break away into the passage by the front door. Suddenly there was a second explosion and Annie collapsed, shot in the back. She died almost immediately.

John stood there, dumbfounded. The shots alarmed a carter, Thomas Smith, who was in the stable attending to the horses. He ran in through the front door to find John screaming for help. Smith calmed John down and told him he was going for the police and the doctor. PC Holliday arrived with Superintendent Bennett. The superintendent had dealt with several shocking scenes of violent death during his career in Newbury but confessed 'I have never seen anything more horrible.'

Dr William Jenner Clarke examined the bodies and shook his head. Superintendent Bennett posted policemen on guard and returned to the police station, taking the gun, which belonged to John Chamberlain, and two spent cartridges.

A message was sent to George Heath, Annie and Sydney's father, at Boames Farm. He and his wife ran to Warren Farm, unable to believe that fate could be so cruel. It was an icy night, and the elderly Mr Heath slipped several times before arriving at the scene of the tragedy.

Once there, the police refused to allow Mrs Heath inside the building, as the sight would be too distressing. Sydney's wife was at first incredulous, then distraught, and had to be comforted by friends and neighbours.

John Chamberlain was nearly frantic with grief, and left the farm, vowing never to step inside the door again. The local paper reported 'The poor fellow seemed quite at a loss to account in any way for the frightful tragedy in which he had just played such a prominent part. It was his gun that had been used, he being in the habit of doing a little rabbit shooting and keeping his gun in the room where the tragedy took place. He was however, always most careful never to allow it to remain loaded whilst indoors, and it was certainly loaded without his knowledge.'

News of the tragedy had spread rapidly, and public curiosity was intense. The house was left exactly as Superintendent Bennett had found it, with a police guard until the following morning, when the inquest was to be heard. A large crowd of pressmen and onlookers had gathered outside The Gun public house nearby, where the coroner, Dr Henry Watson, had decided to hold the inquest. He and the jury walked up to Warren Farm to see for themselves the terrible scene of the night before. Things did not go well from the start. The building had been locked up and the key given to Superintendent Bennett. Unfortunately, the door had two locks and there was no sign of the second key. One of the jurors broke a window pane and a policeman got through the window to open the door. The coroner said afterwards 'I have never seen a more sickening sight.'

The jury walked back to the Gun pub to hear the evidence. The question on everyone's lips was 'How could the woman shoot herself in the back with a shotgun?' It was a long-barrel gun which stood taller than she did. Dr Watson set about trying to establish the truth of the matter. He heard evidence that Annie Chamberlain was of unsound mind. This surprised the local people, who knew her as an amiable and cheerful woman, courteous to all and a regular churchgoer. But, she had left a suicide note. It was tinged in black and largely incoherent. For some reason, she blamed

Warren Farm near Newbury was the scene of violent death in 1891 (photograph by Peter Bloodworth).

her mother. 'You have made our lives a misery to us all,' it read. 'This action I have done as a means of release from it. Hoping you will forgive me.'

Her father could offer no explanation for the letter, and pointed out that the family was a close and loving one. But he had noticed his daughter behaving oddly in recent weeks. The coroner asked him 'Can you tell us anything of the state of her mind?' Mr Heath replied 'Latterly, there has been something that weighed on her nerves. I have never heard her give expression to any threat, but other members of the family have. I have no doubt that her mind was slightly unhinged. I asked the husband about it yesterday, but the answer did not seem quite satisfactory.' John Chamberlain followed him into the witness box. He was in a highly distressed state, sobbing loudly, with the added burden of trying to explain how his wife had met her death in such strange and violent circumstances.

Was the story of him being asked to leave the room a carefully constructed alibi? Or was there some terrible secret between brother and sister which Annie wanted concealed forever? Did her brother know something so awful that she was determined to silence him to stop the family skeletons from getting out of the cupboard? The jury listened intently to what John Chamberlain had to say.

'I rushed into the room and she was standing there before the fire, with the muzzle directed towards herself,' he told the court. 'I made a rush at my wife and seized hold of the stock and begged her to kiss me. She began screaming and looked as wild as could be. She dashed by me towards the door, and I tried with every effort to wrest the gun away from her. She had kept her hold on the muzzle, and I had hold of the stock. She rushed towards the passage, holding the gun as tight as death, and scrambled into a corner. I made a desperate effort to try and get the gun away, but by some means the gun exploded.'

At this point, he broke down completely, laid his head on the table and sobbed hysterically. When he recovered sufficiently to continue, he told the coroner the gun was never loaded in the house and that cartridges were always kept separately. Annie must have had the gun ready and loaded. That, together with the suicide note, ruled out the possibility of an accident. Chamberlain went on to say his wife's behaviour had become very odd. 'One night after supper, I noticed her very strange in her manner,' he said in his low, faltering voice. 'After she got to bed, she put her head at the bottom of the bed and her feet up on the pillow.' He confirmed the suicide note was definitely Annie's handwriting. 'Are you quite sure the gun was empty?' asked the coroner. Chamberlain replied that he had checked it that morning, and it was not loaded. He did not know if Annie had ever learned how to use a gun, but admitted she could easily have had access to ammunition. 'I kept my cartridges in the cupboard, and there were some on the mantel shelf,' he said. 'I placed 20 there on Thursday morning to return to Mr Jackson, from whom I had borrowed some. There was not time to load the gun – it must have been already loaded and cocked.'

The coroner aimed a series of questions to try and establish how Annie could possibly have been shot in the back. 'I could not say how it occurred, she held the barrel with deathly power,' said Chamberlain. Then, almost mumbling, 'I may have touched the trigger myself in the struggle.'

The coroner called Dr Clarke, who had attended the scene of the tragedy. He told the jury Annie had consulted him a few months previously, when she had a miscarriage.

'She suffered from debility afterwards, and seemed to me to be of a highly nervous temperament, but beyond that there was nothing unusual in her condition,' he said. He confirmed that John Chamberlain's account of how Annie met her death was quite possible. He said there was no doubt in his mind that death was caused by a gunshot wound accidentally inflicted during the struggle.

The coroner turned to the jury and asked if they wanted a post mortem examination on Mrs Chamberlain. The foreman, Mr Philip Wells Jackson, said he was not satisfied that the whole story had been told. 'There seems to be something in the background,' he said. But Dr Clarke insisted that a post mortem would throw no further light on the subject, and most of the jurors took the view that Annie would have shot herself anyway whether she struggled with her husband or not. The jury retired to consider.

After some consultation over the wording, the jury returned its verdict 'That Annie Maria Chamberlain was accidentally shot by a double-barrelled gun whilst her husband was endeavouring to take it away from her, to prevent her from committing suicide.'

'That Sydney George Heath was shot by his sister with a double-barrelled gun, and that at the time she was suffering under temporary derangement.'

The coroner referred to the suicide note, and asked the witnesses if there had been trouble in the family. The answers prompted him to say 'Well, there was some family trouble, and where is the family that there is not.'

Brother and sister were buried a few days later in the churchyard at Enborne, where several generations of the Heath family are interred. A large number of people came to pay their last respects, most of them gathered at the church gate, as the two coffins took up most of the space in the tiny church. A deep grave had been dug in the churchyard, and first Sydney, then Annie, were lowered into it.

Foremost among the mourners was John Chamberlain, who was by now the subject of intense press speculation. It turned out he was not who everyone thought he was. He was born Moses Belcher Whitehorn, and his parents had kept the Blackbird pub at Bagnor, on the other side of Newbury. They died when he was very young, and Moses was adopted by his mother's sister, the wife of Mr Benjamin Chamberlain, a local farmer and dealer. When Benjamin died, he left Moses £3,000 – a very large sum in those days – on condition that he changed his name to John Chamberlain, which he promptly did.

He was also the beneficiary of Annie's will. Dr Clarke had now admitted that he had examined Annie two weeks before her death, because her husband had taken out an insurance policy on her life for a 'very large sum'. Public speculation put the figure at £50,000, but Chamberlain never disclosed the true amount.

This excited local curiosity to fever pitch, and the tragedy was the subject of much discussion for a long time afterwards. No-one could prove that John Chamberlain was not telling the truth, but if he wasn't, he was an extremely accomplished actor.

John Chamberlain refused to set foot in the house ever again, and it stood empty for some time. It was later bought by Captain Tredinnick, who farmed the land for many years. Today, Warren Farm stands derelict, waiting to be demolished. Deserted and unfit for habitation, the solidly built mid-Victorian house has slowly crumbled to its death, as if crying for shame for the terrible events that once took place there.

THE LADY KILLER
OF NEWBURY

IN 1892, a young man by the name of Ellis Wynn came to Newbury to work as an assistant in the jewellery shop owned by Mr Garlick. Wynn was a personable young man in his mid-twenties, and made many friends in the town. He was also very much a 'Walter Mitty' character, and told everyone he met that he was of independent means, and only worked in the jeweller's shop because it amused him to do so. He hinted he was about to become the beneficiary of a relative's will, and announced his intention to travel the world and settle in Australia.

Such a young man was bound to turn the pretty heads of Newbury's ladies, and he soon struck up a friendship with a girl who worked in a Mr Jackson's drapery establishment in the Market Place.

Like Wynn, Miss Edith Stevens had come to Newbury to work. He came originally from Tonbridge in Kent, and she came from Watford at the age of 21 to work at the draper's. Wynn decided to leave his job at the jeweller's, and said he was about to go on his world trip, with Naples as his first port of call.

In May, 1892, he left town, but only for a few days. He then returned to see his sweetheart. They spent the day at Savernake Forest, and both returned home very happy. It was a Sunday, and the couple visited friends in Craven Road. As the evening wore on, Miss Stevens decided to stay the night at her friends' house. After the womenfolk had retired to bed, Wynn stayed up talking with his friend, Mr Francis Andrews. Wynn's mood changed, and he became anxious and plaintive. He complained of having severe headaches, and confided to Mr Andrews that he intended to shoot himself. Apparently it had transpired that the relative from whose will Wynn expected to receive a large inheritance had in fact cut him off without a penny. Wynn's boast of independent means was a sham. He had no money of his own and was deeply in debt.

Andrews was alarmed at his friend's state of mind. He took the suicide threat seriously, and on searching Wynn's pockets, found a revolver. He took it from him and locked it away.

Next morning, Miss Stevens went to her place of work as usual, after arranging to meet Wynn later. For his part, his mood had returned to normal, and he was smiling and cheerful to all the people he met in the town during the day. He went round saying goodbye to his friends, telling them all he was about to embark on his travels. It was as if the conversation with Andrews the previous evening had never happened. Wynn told Andrews he felt much better, and wanted to take the revolver back to the friend in Reading from whom he had borrowed it. Andrews had kept it locked up, along with ammunition he had taken from Wynn's coat pocket. Wynn's sunny disposition convinced Andrews it was safe to give him back the gun, and he handed it over.

That evening, Wynn met Edith Stevens as she finished work at the draper's shop. The two walked arm in arm through the town, in the company of one of Miss Stevens' colleagues, Miss Lizzie Pecover. She left them at the junction

of Enborne Road and walked home. She was the last one to
see either of them alive. The couple walked down to the lane
leading to Enborne Gate Farm.

There, Wynn drew the revolver from his pocket and shot
his sweetheart in the back. As she collapsed, he shot her
again, twice in the head. She died instantly. Then he put the
barrel of the revolver in his mouth and pulled the trigger.
The shot blew his brains out, and he fell dead in the road.

It was dusk as shepherd John Quelch heard three shots.
There was a pause, then another. Sergeant Edmund Holding
was on foot patrol in the town centre. As he walked down
Enborne Road from the town centre, he thought he heard a
shot. His pace quickened as he went to investigate, and he
arrived at the scene at the same time as Quelch the shepherd.
The bodies lay in a pool of blood, the gun still tightly
clutched in the young man's hand. Sgt. Holding sent for
help, and Superintendent George Bennett soon arrived with
two doctors. Superintendent Bennett took the five-shot
English Bulldog revolver from the dead man's hand, and
ordered the bodies to be moved to some nearby farm
buildings.

An inquest was held next day at the farm, and doctors
performed a post mortem on the deceased. The jury
inspected the bodies and listened to the evidence of Dr
William Jenner Clarke. He told them 'We examined the
woman and confined our examination to where the shot
wounds were. There was a good deal of blood about the
face, more especially round the nose and mouth. There was
a hole in the skull on the left side, on the top of the head,
and the brain was protruding. The jaw was found to be
completely shattered. The gun must have been fired into her
open mouth. Another bullet was found in the brain, having
fractured the skull just above the right ear.

One of the jurors asked 'Did she scream?' Dr Clarke replied 'That I cannot say. The shots were fatal.'

He said he then examined the body of the man. 'The mouth showed signs of scorching, and I have no doubt that the weapon was fired directly into the mouth,' he said. 'The bullet went through the roof of the mouth, the centre and base of the skull, the middle of the brain, and out of a hole at the top of the head. Death was instantaneous.'

The coroner refused to hear evidence of where Wynn had bought the gun, and criticised the fact that, in those days, they were so freely available. 'They can be bought easily for a few shillings,' he said. The jury heard evidence that Wynn could have been of unsound mind, but the coroner directed them that they were required to return a verdict of how the young couple died, and that the state of Wynn's mind was not relevant to that. The jury duly found that Wynn was guilty of the murder of Miss Stevens and had then committed suicide.

The bodies were taken to the mortuary at the back of the Corn Exchange, where a large crowd gathered to look through an air-brick to see the corpses laid out on a slab. Wynn's body lay there for several days – covered only with an old sack – as a row broke out over who would pay for his burial. A gold pocket watch had been found on him, but it turned out this was borrowed from a friend, who had subsequently claimed it back. This prevented Superintendent Bennett from selling the watch to defray the burial expenses. Eventually, some of Wynn's acquaintances held a collection, and the body was secretly removed from the mortuary at midnight and taken to the cemetery chapel in a coffin of plain elm with black handles. He was buried without ceremony at dawn, with only a few mourners present. The grave was immediately filled in, and no marker was left.

Edith Ethel Stevens made her last journey by train to her home town of Watford, where she was given a Christian burial.

The spot where the couple met such a violent death had meanwhile become a place of morbid interest and hundreds of people went to visit the site of the gruesome killing, marked by a cross cut in the turf at the side of the road.

By now, Wynn's past had caught up with him. Much evidence of his odd behaviour was now becoming available. Instead of the well-to-do young man-about-town, it turned out his parents were divorced and that as a small boy, Wynn had delighted in keeping snakes in his pocket. The most damning statement, made by someone who had known him as a child in Kent, said 'His father tried to kill his mother by cutting her throat. He was sentenced to 20 years' penal servitude.'

THE CASE OF THE
KINDLY FOSTER MOTHER

ABARGEMAN was slowly navigating his craft along the Kennet near Reading in 1896. He brought up a small parcel from the water on the end of his pole. What he discovered in the parcel was to uncover murder on a huge scale.

To his horror, he found it contained the body of a baby girl. She had been strangled with a cord around her neck, and there was a brick to weigh the package down. He moored the barge and went for the police. Detectives came and examined the parcel with particular thoroughness. It was taken away to the police station in Reading for forensic examination, and the bargeman continued on his way. The inspection of the parcel and the body inside it were the first steps in a lengthy and painstaking case which was to shock the whole world.

The parcel had only been in the water for a few days, and on the brown paper was the faint outline – almost obliterated by its immersion – of some writing. It was an address. Police were able to decipher the name 'Mrs Dyer', with an address at Piggotts Road, near the river in Caversham. It was their first clue.

A specially-picked squad of police was sent to surround the house and arrest the occupants. They were too late. Mrs

Dyer had already moved on, and the house was empty.

Reading Borough Police were joined by Scotland Yard. Dozens of tiny bodies had been found in the Thames to the west of London over the past year. A large police operation got quickly into gear, based at Reading police station. Although the address in Caversham had proved a failure, detectives traced Mrs Dyer to a house in West Reading.

Superintendent Tewsley ordered the river to be dragged, and the house in West Reading to be raided.

The squad which had been deployed at Caversham surrounded Mrs Dyer's house in Kensington Road, near Battle Hospital, in Oxford Road. There they found vast quantities of baby clothes and tickets from pawnbrokers which showed how she had disposed of even more. There were hundreds of letters from people answering adverts offering to adopt children for a fee in papers all over the country. There was a nine year old boy named William Thornton, a girl called Oliver, aged eight, and a baby in the house. All were taken into care. The police dug up the garden, but found nothing.

Now, teams of police were searching through newspapers to find 'foster mother' adverts. They found dozens, from as far apart as Bristol and London. There had been adverts in Cheltenham, Gloucester, Newcastle-upon-Tyne, Stafford and small towns across the south of England. The police were now aware of the magnitude of the crimes committed by Mrs Dyer.

She had developed over the years a scam that was to earn her a fortune. She had started in Bristol with an advert in the local paper, offering to adopt children for a fee. In those difficult times, women would hand over small children, thinking they were to be well looked after. It was a better fate than the workhouse, so they thought, and gladly paid

WANTED at once RAKE-HANDLE
MAKER. — Apply, R. DEVERALL,
Sandy Lane, Chippenham, Wilts.

WANTED, young lady APPRENTICE to the
General Drapery, outdoor. — Apply,
Messrs. BEALE & LEATE, 14, Bartholomew-
street.

WANTED care of a NURSE CHILD, would
have good home, healthy neighbourhood,
good references can be given.—Apply A.B.,
Post Office. Aldworth, Reading.

WANTED two respectable girls, one as
HOUSEMAID, the other as KITCHEN-
MAID.—Mrs. JONES, 31, Grand Parade,
Eastbourne.

An advertisement in the Newbury Weekly News for foster babies.
They were to meet a cruel fate.

Mrs Dyer between £10 and £20 – more in some cases –
along with all the child's clothing.

This was a much less squeamish age than our own.
Illegitimacy was rife, and there was no birth control, no free
abortions, no state benefits for children. Working class
single mothers had the choice of sending their babies to the
orphanage, or handing them over to a foster mother – with
as much cash as they could raise.

Mrs Dyer always promised to keep in touch with the
mothers – but never did.

The babies were all murdered, and as soon as anxious
mothers started to get awkward, Mrs Dyer moved on. She
lived all over the country under a string of false names, and

on two occasions – when things got a bit too hot for her – managed to get herself certified insane and into an asylum. As soon as the heat was off, she got herself discharged. She would then go into business in another town, but with the same modus operandi, even selling the baby clothes that came with each of her victims.

In 1895, she came to Berkshire, and a slightly sinister advert appeared in the *Newbury Weekly News:* 'Wanted, care of a nurse child, would have good home, healthy neighbourhood; good references can be given. Apply A.B., Post Office, Aldworth'. It is possible that the woman was using the name Barber at this stage, hence the initials 'A.B.'. The Christian names she usually used were Amelia or Annie.

Superintendent Tewsley knew he had enough evidence to put Dyer on trial. The real headache was the sheer scale of her crimes. His police team was to be busy for a long time, unravelling the complicated web that Dyer had spun.

Vehemently denying she had done anything wrong, she was arrested and charged with murder.

The original charge sheet is preserved at the Thames Valley Police museum at Sulhamstead, along with some of the letters she wrote. Her writing was in the usual copperplate style used at the time, but in an ill-educated manner, with numerous spelling mistakes and very poor grammar. The police kept a number of other gory items, such as a lock of her mousy hair.

Mrs Dyer was initially charged with only one murder, that of Helena Fry, daughter of one Mary Fry. Mrs Dyer was arrested on April 3, 1896, by Reading Constabulary, and charged as Annie Dyer, alias Thomas, alias Harding, aged 57 of Kensington Road, Reading. The charge sheet records her occupation as 'nurse'. She was accused that she 'did wilfully and with malice aforethought, kill and murder a certain female infant, Helena Fry, daughter of one Mary Fry'.

The police started to drag the Kennet and the Thames. Within days, more bodies were found. One was a little boy tied up in a linen wrapper, weighted with a heavy stone. Another was in canvas, tied the same way, weighed down with a brick. Two more were in a carpet-bag which was identified as Mrs Dyer's. Again, bricks were used as weights.

By now the story was making headlines in the press, and police were besieged with hundreds of letters from distraught mothers. They came from all over the country and had entrusted their children to the care of the dastardly Mrs Dyer.

The Reading coroner called an inquest into the deaths of the six babies found in the river. An 11-month old boy found in the carpet bag was identified as the child of Mrs Lizzie Simmonds, a ladies' maid who lived at Ealing. She had given the boy to a Mrs Annie Harding, of Kensington Road, Reading, along with £10 and some clothes, which were later found at Dyer's home.

The baby girl found by the bargeman was identified as Doris Marnon, daughter of a barmaid from Cheltenham, Evelina Edith Marnon. She had seen an advert in a Bristol paper, and at the end of March, Mrs Dyer, alias Mrs Harding, went to Cheltenham to fetch the child – and the £10 premium. She promised Miss Marnon she would write to say how the child was getting on, but the only letter she got was one from the police, asking her to come to Reading.

Thinking there was something amiss, and that she would have to take her daughter home again, Evelina Marnon arrived at Reading with a shawl to wrap her in. She collapsed with grief when police told her of her daughter's fate and asked her to identify the body.

Dyer appeared before a packed Reading Borough Police Court on Saturday, April 11th, for the first of many trial appearances. Her son-in-law, Arthur Ernest Palmer, had been arrested at his home in Mayo Road, Willesden, and charged with being an accessory.

Dyer stood in the dock, all dressed in black and carrying a black and white plaid shawl. Palmer was aged about 30, and said nothing. Prosecutor Mr Sydney Brain applied for a remand in custody, on the grounds that police investigation was continuing. The chairman of the bench asked Mrs Dyer why she should not be held in custody and she replied 'I don't know.' Both prisoners were taken down and remanded for seven days in Reading prison. Mrs Dyer refused to tell the police anything – except that she didn't want a lawyer because it would be too expensive.

By now the evidence being gathered by police was considerable. Over 40 infant bodies had been found in the Thames, and there was proof that Mrs Dyer had received 17 babies in the past three months.

Prison life did not agree with her, and she began to crack. On April 16th, she was given prison notepaper to write a confession to Superintendent Tewsley, and a letter to her son-in-law. She said her daughter and son-in-law, Arthur Ernest Palmer, had nothing to do with any of the deaths. She also wrote to Arthur to tell him of her confession.

'How my heart aches for you and my dear Polly,' she wrote. 'I am writing this to tell you I have eased my mind and made a full statement, and have told them the truth, and nothing but the whole truth, as I hope to be forgiven. God almighty is my judge, and I dare not go into his presence with a lie. I do hope and pray God will forgive me. I had a letter from Polly, she is coming down to see me. She will have a lawyer, but for myself, it is only throwing money away. I

Mrs Dyer, foster mother and murderess.

know I have done this awful thing and I know that I alone will have to answer for it. I hope God will give you both grace and strength to bear this awful trial. God bless you my dear boy, your broken hearted mother.'

She stood again in the dock at Reading with Palmer on Saturday, April 18th, to face additional charges of the murders of Doris Marnon, found by the bargeman, and Harry Simmonds, found in the carpet bag dragged from the Thames at Caversham Weir. Again the prosecution asked for an adjournment because further evidence was expected.

Evelina Marnon appeared in court with the letter Mrs Dyer had written to persuade her to part with her baby and £10 in cash. It read:

'I should be glad to have a dear little girl, one I could bring up and call my own,' she wrote. 'First I must tell you we are plain, homely people, in fairly good circumstances. We live in our own house. I have a good and comfortable home. We are in the country, and sometimes I am alone a great deal. I do not want a child for money's sake, but for company and home comfort. Myself and husband are dearly fond of children. I have no child of my own. A child with me will have a good home, and a mother's love and care. We belong to the Church of England. Although I want to bring up the child as my own, I should not mind the mother, or any person coming to see the child at any time. It would be a satisfaction to see and know the child was going on all right. I only hope we may come to terms.'

Little Doris Marnon never made it to Reading. Dyer took her straight to Palmer's home at Willesden and strangled her. The next morning she took the train from Paddington with the tiny body in the carpet bag. By nightfall, Doris was in a parcel at the bottom of the river.

The case was again adjourned, and both prisoners held in

custody. Their next appearance, the following Saturday, was to be the turning point in the case. The police produced witnesses to testify that children had appeared at Mrs Dyer's addresses at Kensington Road, Piggotts Road, and Elm Villas, Lower Caversham. None of the infants was ever seen again. Mr Albert Charles Culham, a carriage cleaner, of May Road, Willesden, said Mrs Dyer paid in advance for her daughter and son-in-law to lodge at his house.

He told how he had had a fireplace moved, and that some surplus bricks were stacked behind the house – some of which he used to support a rabbit hutch and the clothes post for his wife's washing line. A detective produced the bricks used to weight some of the bodies found in the river. Culham nodded, and confirmed they had come from his house.

Dyer was aware of the keen media interest in her, and tried to sell her story to the papers. Although prison censorship prevented her from doing so, she managed to contact a journalist, who published her confession in the London daily papers. She made it clear she would plead insanity, and might attempt suicide. 'I should certainly kill myself if I had the opportunity,' she said, going on to say that she considered her circumstances gave her good grounds for an insanity plea. She had been an inmate at both Gloucester and Wells asylums, and had attempted to commit suicide at Bristol, and her mother had died in an asylum. 'I have been very bad in my head since my arrest,' she said.

A few days later, the coroner's court recorded a verdict of 'wilful murder' on the first three bodies pulled out of the river, and Mrs Dyer appeared for the last time before Reading magistrates on May 2nd, 1896. By now, yet another body had been found in the river, this time at Sonning. It was a little boy, badly decomposed, and made a total of seven. Police brought it to headquarters in Reading and an inquest was held next day.

The crowd waited outside the police court where Mrs Dyer was making her last appearance. She preserved her usual stolid composure, sitting with her eyes fixed on her lap and saying nothing. At the insistence of her daughter, she had a solicitor and two barristers representing her.

Palmer sat in the dock 'looking like a city clerk on a night out'. To everyone's surprise, the prosecution offered no evidence against Palmer, and he was released from custody.

The court was then told of Dyer's confession, written while she was in Reading prison. Despite objections from Mr Kapadia, Dyer's counsel, the letter was read out:

'To the Superintendent of Police.
Sir, Will you kindly grant me the favour of presenting this to the magistrates. I have made this statement out, for I may not have the opportunity then. I must relieve my mind. I do know and feel my days are numbered on this earth, but I do feel it is an awful thing, drawing innocent people into trouble. I do know I shall have to answer before my Maker in heaven for the awful crimes I have committed, but as God almighty is my judge in heaven, as on earth, neither my daughter, Mary Ann Palmer, nor her husband, Arthur Ernest Palmer, had anything to do with it. They never knew I contemplated such a wicked thing until it was too late. I am speaking the truth and nothing but the truth, as I hope to be forgiven. I myself, and I alone, must stand before my Maker in heaven to give answer for it all. Witness my hand, Amelia Dyer.'

As the clerk of the court finished reading the letter, Mrs Dyer showed her first sign of emotion. At the mention of her daughter's name, she buried her face in her hands and wept.

Mr Kapadia commenced his attempt at an insanity plea by suggesting the letter had been written while the prisoner was of unsound mind. The bench rejected his application, saying the prisoner's mental state would be determined by a judge and jury.

Amelia Dyer was committed for trial at the Old Bailey. She was taken from the police court to the prison, and from there to Reading station. Handcuffed to a wardress, she was put on the London train to be transferred to Holloway Prison. She was never to see Reading again.

Meanwhile, Arthur Palmer had been re-arrested. After his surprise release from court, he was handed over to police at Devonport. There he was charged as Alfred Ernest Palmer, alias Alfred Parsons, alias Alfred Potson, with wilfully abandoning a child, Queenie Baker, at Devonport. He appeared before the town's magistrates, and with an even stranger twist of fate, pleaded guilty. He was sentenced to three months' hard labour.

Mrs Dyer's case came to the Central Criminal Court in May, 1896. The courtroom was packed with curious people, including dozens of newspaper reporters, there to cover the story. Some papers brought out special editions, just with the result of the day's trial. The evidence was overwhelming, and the whole thing was over very quickly. It was feared Mrs Dyer might try to kill herself, and she was kept under close observation at Holloway, with two female warders watching her during the day, and three at night. She was examined by two doctors whilst in prison, and defence lawyers tried hard to convince the jury that she was insane. Mr Kapadia called a Dr Logan, of Bristol, who had committed Dyer to an asylum two years previously. He told the court she was violent and suffering from delusions. She had told him she heard voices in her head, and that the birds whispered to her.

The jury would have none of it. It took them five minutes to return their verdict of 'Guilty of wilful murder'.

Mr Justice Hawkins pronounced sentence of death, and said he was satisfied she had 'carried on her wicked trade for a very long time'. He asked her why such a sentence should not be passed, but Mrs Dyer made no reply.

She was taken to Newgate prison to await the gallows, in company with three other murderers. Despite the heavy security, she made two attempts at suicide, the second almost succeeding. She pretended to be asleep, and tried to strangle herself under the blanket. She was a powerful woman, and the two wardresses in her cell only succeeded in preventing her at the last minute.

The executioner, James Billington, came to Newgate to execute the three male prisoners and Dyer. Billington put Dyer on the weighing scales – necessary to see how far she would have to drop to ensure that death was instant, about five feet in this case. She was aged 57, and weighed 15 stones.

Dyer retired to rest in an agitated state of mind and passed a very restless night. The chaplain came to the condemned cell early in the morning, followed later by the governor and the under-sheriff. Shortly before nine o'clock on the morning of Wednesday, June 10th, 1896, James Billington came to pinion her, ready for the scaffold. Billington was worried that her heavy weight might cause her body to split open when she dropped from the trap, and he took special care to ensure she stayed intact. He did this in the presence of five female warders, all of whom knew Dyer might make trouble. She had told one of them 'I will never walk to the scaffold.' She was as good as her word. A newspaper report of the time said 'The convict seemed in a dazed condition, and had to be

supported by female officers. The distance from the cell to
the drop was only a few yards. The convict was quickly
placed in position beneath the beam, and the noose and cap
were at once adjusted by Billington, his assistant rapidly
performing the other preparations, the convict being
meanwhile supported by the warders. The hangman pulled
the lever, the drop fell without any hitch, and the wretched
woman died instantly.'

DEATH OF A TROOPER

THE scarlet tunic of a soldier who was hanged for the murder of his wife was the inspiration for Oscar Wilde's *Ballad of Reading Gaol*. The soldier was Trooper Charles Wooldridge, who was executed at the prison in 1896. Wooldridge grew up in the village of East Garston on the Lambourn Downs, where he spent his boyhood. He was an ambitious lad, and wanted to see the world. The way to do that, a century ago, was to join the army, and his family was proud of him when he was accepted for the Royal Horse Guards. He had grown up with horses, and was just the sort of recruit the elite cavalry unit was looking for.

Although the regiment saw action on many occasions overseas, it was also required to fulfil ceremonial functions, and Wooldridge soon found himself on guard duty at Windsor Castle.

Off-duty soldiers were allowed a certain amount of freedom in the town, and thus it was that the young trooper met his future wife Nell. She worked in the post office at Clewer village, tucked between Windsor and the racecourse. She was, by all accounts, a spirited young woman. From the start, the relationship was stormy, but the couple married and tried to make a go of it.

Trooper Wooldridge was posted to London. He was now just turned 30, and wanted to settle down, but Nell had become used to living alone. She was a flirt, and did not shun the company of other soldiers while her husband was away.

Wooldridge was stationed at Hyde Park Barracks for guard duty at Buckingham Palace when Queen Victoria was in residence, and for other ceremonial duties. He was devastated when stories of Nell's infidelities reached him, and decided to go absent without leave to try and sort things out with her. He loved Nell with the sort of blind passion that makes men's minds and hearts explode into reckless violence – knowing what the result of their actions will be, but caring nothing for the inevitable consequences. Wooldridge could not live without Nell, and he was determined that if he couldn't have her, then no other man would.

He had been to see her a few days previously, but the visit ended in a blazing row, with him knocking her to the floor in a blaze of anger. He blamed himself for losing his temper, but claimed she had provoked him intolerably. She promised to come and see him at the barracks, but never turned up. Wooldridge asked the sentry to look out for her, and to let him know if she came. He told the soldier 'If she does not come today, I must go to Windsor. I want to see her very particular. I must go, and come back by the last train – for I am going to do some damage.'

Desperate to sort the situation out, he left the barracks without permission and took the train to Windsor. He arrived at the house where Nell was lodging, and was shown into her room. Wooldridge was still hoping to work things out, but had decided this was the last chance. Again Nell unleashed her spiteful tongue on him, goading him, totally regardless of his feelings for her. It was more than he could stand. In a fit of blind rage, he took his razor from his pocket. He could take no more, and with a fatal sweep he cut Nell's throat. Her death was mercifully swift, and no sooner had Wooldridge realised the awful finality of his reckless action than the police were on the scene, to find him with Nell's body, still with blood on his hands. He was perfectly sober, and made no attempt to escape.

Trooper Wooldridge was taken into custody at Windsor police station, and appeared before the town's magistrates, charged with murder. 'I am not guilty,' he told the court, and his lawyer tried to get the charge reduced to manslaughter, because of the provocation he had endured. But the bench would have none of it, and the prisoner was committed to Reading Assizes to be tried by judge and jury.

The jury strongly recommended mercy because of the element of provocation, but that did not stop the trial judge, Mr Justice Hawkins, from putting on the black cap to sentence Wooldridge to death.

The local paper reported 'Hopes were entertained that he would be reprieved, but the Home Secretary declined to interfere.'

Trooper Wooldridge faced the death sentence with calmness, saying he deserved it. He expressed sorrow for taking Nell's life, and told the chaplain at Reading Gaol, Rev M T Friend, that he hoped to meet her in heaven.

Wooldridge spent the final weeks of his life resigned to his fate. He was allowed out for exercise each day, and sat on the little patch of grass at the edge of the prison yard to smoke his pipe.

The poet and playwright Oscar Wilde, Reading Gaol's most famous prisoner, could see the yard from his cell window, and watched Wooldridge with dreadful fascination. The story of the soldier's crime, and of his impending doom, was well known to all the prisoners. Wilde was deeply affected, even though the two men never met and were not allowed to speak.

Wilde had just lost a sensational libel action against the Marquess of Queensbury, founder of the modern sport of boxing. He was convicted of being a homosexual – a crime carrying a term of imprisonment in those days – and locked up at Reading Gaol. It was inevitable that the tall, handsome guardsman would catch his poet's imagination. He records in the ballad that he first saw Wooldridge when the two men were in different parties in the exercise yard.

> 'I walked, with other souls in pain,
> Within another ring
> And was wondering if the man had done
> A great or little thing,
> When a voice behind me whispered low,
> "That fellow's going to swing."
>
> I only knew what hunted thought
> Quickened his step and why
> He looked upon the garish day
> With such a wistful eye;
> The man had killed the thing he loved,
> And so he had to die.'

The Ballad shows that Wilde never met Wooldridge, but there can be no doubt he was obsessed with the soldier's impending execution. Wilde demonstrated a morbid fascination with death in general, and Wooldridge's in particular. Wooldridge was the only man to be executed at Reading when Wilde was there.

Wilde's cell was in C Block, cell C3.3, on a first floor landing. It has been re-numbered C2.2, because the first cell on the landing has been converted into a lavatory. Otherwise

Aerial view of Reading Gaol. Trooper Wooldridge who was executed here, was the inspiration for Oscar Wilde's poem 'The Ballad of Reading Gaol'.

it is unchanged, apart from new sanitary arrangements intended to avoid the degredation of 'slopping out'.

The view from Wilde's cell, which is about 8 feet by 12 feet, is of the prison yard, down to the trees on the north bank of the river Kennet. The window was more than 6 feet off the ground, less than 2 feet square, and the only way to see out of it is to stand on a chair. Wilde feared he would go mad in C3.3, or that he would lose his sight and senses. He was registered as unfit for hard labour, and was excused from oakum picking, the usual employment allocated to prisoners in their cells. This was the task of unwinding old ropes to be mixed with tar for caulking ships' timbers. It was an effective sealant, but the prisoners hated the job because it wore away the skin of their fingers.

Wilde relieved his mind-numbing existence by looking out of the tiny window, and was inspired by Wooldridge's calm fortitude.

Shortly before the execution was to take place, Wilde looked out of his window to see other prisoners digging a grave in the little grassy patch where Wooldridge was accustomed to sitting in the sunshine with his pipe.

The execution was to be carried out in the photographing room, which had been built as a first floor extension in 1870, when photographing of inmates was first introduced at the gaol. It was brick built, with a glass roof, and as each new prisoner was brought in, he would have his picture taken. A Reading photographer, Thomas Wood of Broad Street, had been granted the contract, and took full face and profile pictures of each prisoner, for the princely sum of one shilling and ninepence – 8.75 pence in today's money. Wilde described it to a friend as 'a little shed with a glass roof, like a photographer's studio on the sands at Margate'.

Public hanging had been abolished in 1868, and the room's grimmer, and less frequent task, was as an execution chamber. In the centre of the floor was a brick-lined pit, 8 feet by 5 feet and 9 feet deep. It was closed with a pair of trap doors secured on the underside by three iron bolts. When released they allowed the doors to open, at which the hapless victim fell to his death. Overhead was a wooden beam from which the noose was suspended. It was first used in March, 1877, to hang the Hungerford police killers, Henry and Francis Tidbury. The prisoners referred to the building as 'the dropping shed.' Although long since demolished, the position of the building can still be clearly seen, and the condemned cell is still there, now used as an office by Berkshire Probation Service, which has a unit inside the prison. The room where the last rites were so grimly intoned to so many men is now home to filing cabinets and a desk-top computer. Wooldridge hoped his father would visit him, and despite his great age, the old man set out on the long journey from East Garston. He arrived at the prison, but was so overwhelmed with grief that he was unable to go on with the terrible ordeal, and had to leave without a final farewell to his unfortunate son.

The hangman arrived at the gaol the day before the execution. James Billington, a barber from Lancashire, had been fascinated by his grim hangman's trade ever since he was a small boy, when he carried out mock executions with dummies on a model gallows. Hangmen usually had an assistant, but Billington was working alone after an unfortunate accident a few weeks previously. His assistant, one Warbrick, had been standing on the trap, and had fallen through it when Billington pulled the lever too early.

Charles Thomas Wooldridge slept well on his last night, July 6th, 1896, and woke for his breakfast at 6 am. Billington went to the condemned cell after the chaplain had finished giving his blessing. The whole of the prison population was straining with dreadful anticipation.

'Trooper Wooldridge walked to the scaffold with that firmness which had characterised his demeanour throughout,' reported a sympathetic local journalist. 'The sad ceremony terminating his life occupied only a few moments.' The customary black flag was hoisted outside the prison to announce Wooldridge's execution. A single bell tolled monotonously at nearby St Laurence's church.

Name *Chas. Thos. Wooldridge*	The length of the drop, as determined before the execution. **6** feet **8** inches.
Register Number *1273*	The length of the drop, as measured after the execution; from the level of the floor of the scaffold to the heels of the suspended culprit. **7** feet **7** inches.
Sex *Male*	Cause of death [(*a*) Dislocation of vertebræ, (*b*) Asphyxia.] *Dislocation of Vertebra*
Age *30*	
Height *5 · 11 3/4*	Approximate statement of the character and amount of destruction to the soft and bony structures of the neck.
Build *prop*	*Muscles much bruised not lacerated much extravasation of blood Complete division of cord Fracture of Sup.t articular processes 3rd Cervical Vertebra Dislocation of 2nd from 3rd*
Weight in clothing (to be taken on the day preceding the execution) *168*	If there were any peculiarities in the build or condition of his neck, which necessitated a departure from the scale of drops, particulars should be stated.
Character of the prisoner's neck *Normal rather long*	*Executioner's attention was called to the scale of drops but he considered a longer drop that 5ft necessary. I do not know of any such peculiarities WM*

The Execution Certificate for Charles Wooldridge.

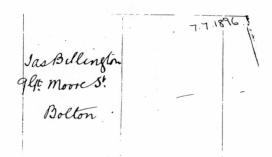

7.7.1896.

Jas Billington
9 Gt. Moore St.
Bolton.

Opinion of the Governor and Medical Officer as to the manner in which each of the above-named has performed his duty.

1. Has he performed his duty satisfactorily ?

   1. Satisfactoryil

2. Was his general demeanour satisfactory during the period that he was in the prison, and does he appear to be a respectable person ?

   2. General demeanour satisfactory The appears a respectable person

3. Has he shown capacity, both physical and mental, for the duty, and general suitability for the post ?

   3. Yes

4. Is there any ground for supposing that he will bring discredit upon his office by lecturing, or by granting interviews to persons who may seek to elicit information from him in regard to the execution or by any other act ?

   4. No

5. Are you aware of any circumstances occurring before, at, or after the execution which tend to show that he is not a suitable person to employ on future occasions either on account of incapacity for performing the duty, or the likelihood of his creating public scandal before or after an execution ?

   5. No.

'The man had killed the thing he loved,
And so he had to die.

And all men kill the thing they love,
By all let this be heard,
Some do it with a bitter look,
Some with a flattering word,
The coward does it with a kiss,
The brave man with a sword!'

Billington did it with a rope and a trap door. Victorian values demanded that a proper record be kept, and the prison still keeps the large book of how executions were conducted. The entries would be comic if they were not so grimly macabre.

Wooldridge's execution certificate shows he was five feet eleven and three-quarter inches tall, with a proportionate build, and weighed 168 pounds. The length of the drop from the trapdoor was calculated at six feet eight inches, but Billington decided to increase it to seven feet seven inches. Death was caused by the 'dislocation of vertebrae', and the prison doctor noted that there was a complete division of the spinal cord.

Wooldridge's body was cut down from the gallows and buried in the prison yard, next to the grave of John Carter, who had had three wives, and murdered them all. It was the last unkindness to Wooldridge, who had dearly loved his wife Nell, but was driven to distraction – and murder – by her infidelity, to be buried next to a man who had cold-bloodedly killed three women.

Oscar Wilde was released from prison in 1897. After a reunion party, organised by friends, Wilde fled to France, never to return to England. He wrote the *Ballad of Reading*

Gaol whilst living in a small hotel at Berneval-sur-Mer, near Dieppe. He described how Wooldridge was driven to distraction by his wife's infidelity and cut her throat with a razor. He dedicated the ballad to Wooldridge.

THE WITCH'S CURSE

T HE hamlet of Heywood Park, in the parish of White Waltham, was a peaceful place until the coming of the Great Western Railway. Then began a whole series of mysterious deaths, culminating in one murder, so bad that the name of the village was eventually changed.

White Waltham got its name because the land belonged to Waltham Abbey, in Essex. The Abbot of Waltham in the year 1275 was a Berkshire man called Reginald de Maidenheth, who had a grudge against a woman whom he accused of being a witch. He ordered her to be arrested, and with no legal authority whatsoever, ordered a gallows to be erected in Cannon Lane in order to hang the woman. The scaffold was duly erected and, cursing the assembled crowd as she went, the poor woman was hanged, without even the semblance of a proper trial. The whole matter was all but forgotten down the centuries, until the coming of the railway, in 1839.

The main line went through from London to Bristol with no problems, but as the railway became more and more heavily used, labourers arrived in White Waltham to build sidings for goods trains. They did not know that long ago a witch had been hanged in Cannon Lane and her body cut down and buried there. The navvies toiled away, unintentionally desecrating the witch's grave and covering it with a steel lattice of railway lines. The labourers finished the job and went away, and everyone was pleased – until the mysterious and bloody deaths started to happen, and local people recalled the almost forgotten piece of folklore about the witch. They attributed these deaths to the witch's curse.

In 1905 John Hussey took the train from Paddington to the West Country. When he got to White Waltham, he got out of his seat as if in a trance, opened the carriage door of the fast-moving train and fell out onto the rails. His corpse, minus a leg, and the contents of his suitcase were found strewn along the track. At the same spot eight years later, a maintenance crew found a decapitated body. It was so badly disfigured it could not be identified. In 1929, the body of Hilda Craig, of Tunbridge Wells, was found on the line – minus her head and arms. The inquest failed to find a reason for her death, even though evidence was given that she suffered from fits of depression. The fatal spot claimed another victim in 1930, when a platelayer was killed after he stepped in front of a train. In 1935, the headless body of William Cullinford of Swindon was found on the track. He was said to be subject to fainting fits and the coroner recorded a verdict of suicide while of unsound mind.

A little further down Cannon Lane, even more horrible things were happening. Milkman Alexander Kirby called the police in April, 1929, to a house where he saw the dead body of a woman through the front window. Officers broke in to find Jessie Goldup with her throat cut and her skull smashed with a hammer. Nearby was her 36 year old husband James, a local baker, who was barely alive and had cut his own throat. He had written a suicide note that he and his wife wanted to die together. He was taken to hospital and recovered, to be found insane and sentenced at Oxford Assizes to be detained at His Majesty's pleasure. Three years later, the curse struck again. In January, 1932, Mrs K

Hawkins arrived at her home in Breadcroft Lane to find the house full of gas fumes and her husband's body on the kitchen floor. He had cut through the gas pipe with a hacksaw and laid down with his head on a pillow.

At the inquest, Mrs Hawkins told the court that her 28 year old husband was a baker by trade, but had been unemployed and was deeply upset by his inability to support his wife and child. There was another verdict of suicide whilst of unsound mind.

Of course deaths occur like these in many areas, but local feeling was that somehow they were connected to the disturbance of the witch's grave.

The catalogue of disasters was to reach its climax in September, 1932, when Ernest Hutchinson moved into the home of Mrs Gwendoline Warren in Heywood Avenue. She was separated from her husband and lived with her 12 year old son, Ronnie. Ronnie had been staying with his aunt at Burnham, and came home one evening to find the house locked, which was unusual. He called the next-door neighbour, a retired policeman by the name of Joseph Hutton, and got in through the kitchen window. The house had been stripped bare, but in the bedroom were the remains of Mrs Warren's bed, dismantled and piled in a heap. Police training was to stand Mr Hutton in good stead. Under the old iron frame was Mrs Warren's body, covered with a mattress and old blankets. She was quite cold.

Hutton immediately called the police, and a manhunt started for Hutchinson, described as 'Aged about 42, height five feet ten inches, wearing grey suit and black shoes. No coat or hat, and carrying an attache case'.

An inquest was opened to enquire into Mrs Warren's death, but adjourned because Hutchinson was being hunted by police, and because the cause of Mrs Warren's death could not be established. Internal organs were sent for forensic examination at a London hospital.

The two officers who took them to London were sent on to Southend-on-Sea, where Hutchinson had been found by Essex police. He was charged with murder by the Berkshire officers and taken to Maidenhead, where he was remanded in custody for one week.

Hutchinson appeared before the Berkshire Assizes at Reading on Friday, October 13th, before His Honour Sir Frank MacKinnon. The inquest had finally recorded that Mrs Gwendoline Annie Warren had been knocked unconscious with a hammer, and then suffocated by the blankets and mattress piled on top of her. She had been dead for several days. Hutchinson, who told the court he was an unemployed baker, pleaded not guilty to the murder charge.

The prosecutor for the Crown, Dr W G Earengey, painted a picture that was to horrify the jury. Hutchinson had sold Mrs Warren's furniture – including a piano – to a dealer called Albert Davis of Bridge Street, Maidenhead, for the paltry sum of 51 shillings, a ridiculously low price. Davis testified in court to that effect, and Mrs Warren's neighbour,

---

FIGHT FOR A LIFE.

The Discovery of a Woman's Body under a Pile of Mattresses

In a Semi-Detached House at Heywood Park.

Accused Man on his Trial at the Berks Assize.

Prisoner Sentenced to Death.

Joseph Hutton, who found her body, said that when he enquired of Hutchinson where she was, he replied that she had gone to Birmingham. Hutchinson had then gone to London and picked up a prostitute called Doris Dew near Waterloo Station. He had given her presents of jewellery – later identified as being Mrs Warren's – and the two had gone off to Southend.

The story Hutchinson told the court was that he was asleep alone on the night of the murder, because Mrs Warren had refused to sleep with him until he got a job. He admitted having an argument with her because he was a heavy smoker, and she resented paying for his habit. He said that after he went to bed, she was downstairs and he heard her open the front door. He said he slept soundly and in the morning got up and made tea for Mrs Warren. 'I brought the tea to Ronnie's bedroom – the bedstead was all thrown up on the bed. I saw a pair of stockinged feet sticking out,' he told the court. He said he did not know what to do. He went out for a cycle ride, and went to the cinema in the evening, leaving Mrs Warren's body untouched in the bedroom. He claimed that Mrs Warren had entertained other men before, and he was sure her death had been caused by one of them. He said that some weeks previously, she had refused to sleep with him and had stayed downstairs. He came down next morning to find her half naked in front of the fire. The back door was open, and there was a man's hat on the dresser. A week later a similar incident occurred and there were two used cups and saucers on the dresser. Hutchinson said he did not make trouble because it was Mrs Warren's house and she could have thrown him out on the street whenever she liked.

He said he did not report Mrs Warren's death because he did not know what to do. 'It is the police's duty to find out

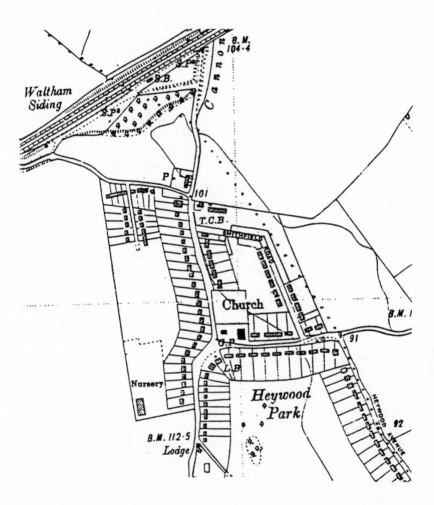

Haywood Park and Waltham Siding before the name was changed to lift the witch's curse.

their own jobs,' he told a hushed courtroom. 'I'm not a lover of the police.'

Judge MacKinnon gave his summing up, accusing Hutchinson, who claimed to have left the body in the house while he went to the pictures, of 'callous brutality'. 'You picked up that wretched prostitute in London and gave her those trinkets,' he said.

The jury reached its verdict after 28 minutes. The judge sat fully robed and wigged as Hutchinson stumbled slightly on the steps up to the dock. He bit his lip as he stood before the tense, silent courtroom, but displayed no other emotion. The Clerk of Assize turned to the jury foreman. 'Are you agreed upon your verdict?' The foreman cleared his throat and whispered 'Guilty'. The Clerk turned to the prisoner and asked him if he had anything to say before sentence was pronounced. Hutchinson swayed slightly, but did not reply. The black cap was placed on the judge's head and the entire court stood in an uncanny silence. Hutchinson clung to the rails of the dock, and a callous smile spread across his face as the judge pronounced sentence of death. Hutchinson continued to smile nonchalantly as he was led away.

Hutchinson walked to the gallows at Oxford Prison, still wearing the callous smile that had become his trademark. He was executed by Alfred Allen, a one-eyed former Provost Sergeant who started his grisly trade with firing squads for deserters in the First World War.

The governor posted the notice of execution on the prison gate. Not a hat was raised as the prison bell tolled.

The events at Heywood Park had caused intense interest for the world's press, and gave the area a somewhat less than salubrious reputation. Suffering worst from this was the local building firm of Cripps and Green, who had just built a new estate of 46 houses and couldn't sell them, because of the adverse publicity. It was decided that the name should be changed from Heywood Park to Woodlands Park. Whether people really believed that changing the name would lift the 'Witch's Curse' is uncertain, but what is certain is that today Cannon Lane is only known for its queues of cars, waiting for the traffic lights under the railway bridge, and Woodlands Park is the peaceful terminus of a suburban bus route.

THE HOUSE OF DEATH

A HOUSE in Walkers Lane, Lambourn was the scene of not only one violent death but two, entirely unconnected, in the space of six years in the 1930s. The first case concerned Derrick Cheshire who was a jockey and stable-lad and worked for a trainer in Lambourn. He lived in Walkers Lane with his common law wife, Miss Gladys Davis, and their four month old baby. Cheshire, aged 27 fell foul of his neighbours, the Giddings family. What began as a silly quarrel was to end in death.

One Sunday evening in the summer of 1930, Cheshire and his wife walked to the Malt Shovel at Upper Lambourn for a drink. She carried her baby in her arms and was looking forward to a break from her domestic chores.

It was not a pleasant evening. Their neighbour Frederick Giddings was in the pub and insulted Miss Davis and Cheshire, who retaliated by striking him. Giddings left, saying 'All right, we will kill you when you get home'. Cheshire took the man at his word, and arranged for other locals to accompany him and his wife. William Clayton, a labourer from Upper Lambourn, was a boxer of some repute. He walked home with the couple with the intention of keeping the peace. As they approached the cottages in Walkers Lane, they saw Frederick Giddings, who was aged 22, and his 29 year old brother Ted sitting on the grass bank outide the cottages, smoking cigarettes.

Clayton approached them and asked Ted if he was waiting for Cheshire. Ted replied that he was doing exactly that. Clayton told Ted that it was not the sort of thing to do and that he should give the fellow a chance. Giddings' reply was to hit him on the nose. Clayton later told the court 'I was struck a heavy blow which put me down. I knew no more until I came round about five minutes later. My nose was bleeding and swollen, my right eye closed, and my head ached. I wiped my eyes and looked around, but could see no-one.'

Clayton missed the terrible scene which occurred in the next few minutes. Cheshire and his wife raced for their cottage door. The Giddings brothers gave chase, snatching up lumps of wood as they ran. Cheshire fumbled desperately for the front door key, but failed. The brothers closed in, brandishing their impromptu cudgels.

'I tried to get away, but I could not, because they were on either side of me,' Cheshire was to tell the court. 'My knife was in my pocket, and I held it up, telling them to keep away.'

He backed off down the garden until cornered in a patch of pea-sticks. The brothers advanced, wielding their fence-posts. Ted Giddings struck out at Cheshire, who lunged at him with the knife, causing a deep wound to his arm. He stepped back, clutching the wound, and his brother came forward with his stick raised. Cheshire lunged again. 'I held the knife in my right hand, and he struck me across the arm,' he told the court 'I saw him fall.'

Cheshire did not wait to see what had happened, he ran straight to the police station. The heavy knife was embedded in Giddings' neck, firmly lodged in the bone.

Sgt. Martin was not at the police house when Cheshire got there, and he blurted out his story to the sergeant's wife. Cheshire had spoken to Sgt. Martin a few days previously, and had asked him for protection against the Giddings brothers. The sergeant had promised to keep an eye on things, and Cheshire had hoped desperately that the policeman was nearby while he had been trying to escape from his attackers.

Dr Bell had run to Walkers Lane, but found the knife so deeply embedded that he judged it dangerous to try and remove it. He decided to send Giddings to hospital for an operation to remove the knife. He took Ted Giddings to his surgery nearby and put three stitches in a knife-wound in his arm. Fred Giddings was completely conscious in the ambulance to Newbury Hospital.

Doctors at Newbury Hospital put Fred Giddings under anaesthetic to remove the knife, which was embedded into the vertebrae of his neck. When he was taken back to the ward after the operation, it was found that he was completely paralysed down his right side. He could not move his arm or leg, and his right lung had collapsed. He died within a week of septic pneumonia – but not before making a deathbed statement, accusing Cheshire of deliberately trying to murder him.

Cheshire had been remanded in custody, charged with maliciously wounding Giddings. Now the charge was murder. The police and magistrates had taken Cheshire to the hospital to take a deposition from Giddings as to his version of events. Fred Giddings was dying, and the police faithfully recorded his deathbed statement, in Cheshire's presence. Cheshire, handcuffed to a policeman, did not speak as Fred Giddings accused him. He was taken to Winchester prison to await trial. Newbury magistrates were having second thoughts about the charge of murder. Cheshire appeared again before the court, and the legal arguments rallied back and forth. Fred Giddings' dying deposition was read out. The story according to the close knit Giddings family was completely different to that told by Cheshire, and magistrates had to sift through the minefield of conflicting evidence. They reduced the charge to manslaughter, and Derrick James Cheshire was committed to Birmingham Assizes for trial.

The judge made short work of the evidence. The case did not start until after the lunchtime recess, and the public prosecutor was dismayed when the judge told him the deathbed evidence of Fred Giddings was inadmissible. The prosecution called Edward Percy Giddings to tell how his brother met his death. Counsel for the defence Mr Donald Hurst ripped into Ted Giddings and demolished his testimony completely. Mr Hurst was instructed by solicitors Charles Lucas and Marshall, and was assisted by Mr Angus Marshall.

Mr Hurst made a solid case that Cheshire had struck out in self-defence. 'As far as you know,' he asked Cheshire, 'was there no other way you could have escaped the blows these men were raining on you?' 'No,' came the reply from Cheshire.

The jury took six minutes to reach their verdict of not guilty, and the prosecution promptly dropped the charge of maliciously wounding Ted Giddings. Cheshire walked free from the court and caught the same train home that evening as the Giddings family and Sgt. Martin. At Oxford, they all got off the train and took the bus home to Lambourn.

Six years later Thomas Townsend and his wife Elizabeth were the tenants of the same cottage formerly occupied by the Giddings family. Thomas Townsend was a simple minded farm worker.

He was 68 years old, and previously he had lived with his family at Sheepdrove, where he worked for a local farmer as a general labourer. He and his wife Elizabeth had been married 20 years. It was her second marriage, and the couple had a stepson, Godfrey Palmer, aged 20, and a daughter, Mary Townsend, aged 17.

Mrs Townsend was an industrious soul, and wanted to

move into the village to be closer to her work. Thomas earned an average of £1.50 per week – and he enjoyed his beer, much to Lizzie's disgust.

She had insisted the family move to Walkers Lane, and she got her way. She was over 20 years younger than her husband, and felt obliged to work to keep the family provided for.

Thomas refused to settle at Walkers Lane. He no longer worked, and approached the superintendent of the workhouse to ask if he could be allowed to live there. His wife was furious, and told the authorities the family had plenty of money – thanks to her hard work – and there was no need for Thomas to apply for poor relief.

One Saturday Elizabeth Townsend went into Newbury for an afternoon's shopping with her daughter Mary, who worked in a cafe, but had the afternoon off. The two had tea together and Mrs Townsend set off back to Lambourn, leaving Mary at the cafe, where she had lodgings. Thomas spent the evening at the George Hotel in Lambourn, where he played dominoes and drank two pints of beer. Witnesses said he left the pub quite sober and went home. When he got there, it was to find his wife in whispered conversation with her son, Godfrey. The conversation ceased when Townsend walked in. Godfrey occupied a curtained-off part of the couple's upstairs bedroom, and mother and son went upstairs to continue their conversation, leaving Townsend downstairs. He sat and waited angrily for Elizabeth to come downstairs. There was a whispered argument, and she opened the door and fled the house. Next door lived Miss Gertrude Cartwright, who owned the row of cottages. She was surprised to hear the sound of running feet on the cobbles, and then a frantic knocking on her door. The latch lifted as Elizabeth Townsend tried desperately to escape her husband, only a step behind her. Miss Cartwright had left a thick woollen draught excluder at

Walkers Lane, Lambourn, where not just one but two separate murders took place in the 1930s (photograph by Peter Bloodworth).

the bottom of the door to keep out the winter wind. It meant Lizzie could not get in.

Miss Cartwright picked up the woollen bundle and threw open the door. Lizzie dashed inside, followed closely by her husband. He was carrying a single barrelled 12-bore shotgun. Before Miss Cartwright could speak, she saw a flash from the muzzle of the gun, and heard the bang as the shot ripped into Lizzie's shoulder. Miss Cartwright stood stunned as Lizzie collapsed in the doorway.

She was bleeding profusely, and Miss Cartwright called for help. Her neighbour Charles Povey and his wife came quickly, and helped Lizzie to a sofa. Povey went for the police, and another neighbour hurried for the doctor. Dr Donald Green lived nearby, and he and his assistant, Dr Spender, ran quickly to the cottage. They worked by the light of an oil lamp in a desperate battle to save the woman's life, but she died three-quarters of an hour later.

The police began the hunt for her husband. Townsend had been seen earlier making off towards Upper Lambourn, and policemen combed the area by torchlight. PC Dixon, the local constable, was returning towards Lambourn when he walked past a derelict barn. A muffled whimper alerted him to the presence of a dog. It was Townsend's. PC Dixon went into the barn and shone his torch. He picked up a stick and began to poke around in the straw on the floor, and within seconds, found Townsend hiding under a pile of straw and rags. He was arrested, taken to Lambourn police station and charged with the murder of his wife. He said to PC Dixon 'I can stand my ground — she got what she asked for.'

Supt. Braby came quickly to the conclusion that Townsend had a very low mentality, which was borne out all through his trial. He stood in the dock at Lambourn police court, saying nothing as the evidence was read out. The *Newbury*

Weekly News described the scene:

'Townsend is a smallish man, slightly bent, five feet four inches in height, with grey hair, sunken features and a sandy-grey moustache,' says the report of the time. 'He was wearing a dark jacket with the collar turned up, a white muffler, corduroy breeches tied with string just below the knees, cloth leggings and heavy, muddy boots.'

He was remanded in custody to face trial at Birmingham Assizes, but was allowed to attend his wife's inquest. He sat silent as the coroner heard evidence of how Mrs Townsend died. Dr Green had performed a post mortem, and told the court she had suffered a gunshot wound to the shoulder. It had been fired at very close range, and the wadding from the cartridge was embedded in her shoulder, along with the fabric of her dress and splinters of bone. She died of shock caused by blood loss.

The case came to court at Birmingham in March. Townsend stood passive in the dock, showing no emotion throughout the day's proceedings, as if it did not concern him in the slightest. The prosecution detailed a damning case against him, against which Newbury solicitor Mr Angus Marshall was unable to defend him. He had instructed barrister Mr Cartwright Sharpe K.C., but all the eloquence in the world did Townsend no good.

'That poor fool in the dock cannot understand ordinary questions, and he makes sheer stupid answers,' Mr Sharpe told the jury. 'He does not know what he is saying. He has the brain power of a little child, with child-like ideas meandering around his head.'

The jury was out for only 20 minutes. Silence fell over the court as they came back to their seats. The clerk asked them 'Are you agreed on your verdict?'

'My Lord,' said the foreman, 'we find the prisoner guilty,

but we wish to make a recommendation of mercy.'

'Is that the verdict of you all?' asked the clerk. The foreman nodded. No-one stirred as the black silk square was placed on the judge's head. All eyes were on him, as Townsend stood in the dock, flanked by warders. He still looked bemused, as if he did not know what was going on.

The clerk spoke to him in measured tones. 'Prisoner at the bar, you have been arraigned on a charge of murder, and have placed yourself upon your country. That country has now found you guilty. Have you anything to say why judgement of death should not be pronounced upon you?'

The white-haired, slightly-built figure stood motionless in the hushed courtroom. He stared at the judge and said nothing. His Lordship broke the silence. 'Is there anything you wish to say?' he asked quietly.

Townsend still stayed silent. After a pause, the warder at his side whispered the question again. Townsend's eyelids flickered. He made to open his mouth, but all he could say was 'No, sir.'

The judge spoke gently to him. 'Thomas Townsend, I have no option but to pass upon you the sentence that the law requires, and that sentence is that you be taken from hence to a lawful prison and thence to a place of execution, and that you be there hanged by the neck until you be dead, and may the Lord have mercy upon your soul.'

Townsend was taken down to the cells as the judge assured the jury their recommendation of mercy would go before the Home Secretary.

His solicitor, Mr Angus Marshall, applied for an appeal, and this was heard in the Court of Criminal Appeal in London in May.

Townsend again stood in the dock, showing no sign of emotion. The appeal was heard by the Lord Chief Justice, Lord

Hewart, with two other judges. Again the defence was unable to get the charge reduced to manslaughter, and the appeal failed. On hearing the verdict, Townsend turned and walked from the dock, accompanied by two warders. He said nothing.

The May 7th edition of the *Newbury Weekly Herald* reported 'Thomas Townsend of Lambourn will be executed on Saturday, May 16 at Birmingham.'

Angus Marshall, who had worked so hard for his poor simple-minded client, was devastated. He had done his best up to the last, sending every scrap of evidence to the Home Secretary in the hope of a reprieve.

He held his head in his hands as he faced the fact that Townsend was to be hanged in a few days time. There was a knock at the door of his office, and his clerk came in with the morning mail. He sighed the resigned sigh of one who has given up all hope. The arrangements were made, the prison chaplain was praying for Townsend, the executioner had weighed and measured him for the drop on the rope that would end his life, and the prison governor had his instructions for the execution.

Angus Marshall picked up a paper knife and idly slit open the first letter on the pile. It was postmarked London, and stamped 'On His Majesty's Service'. Marshall's pulse quickened. He ripped the letter from its envelope and ran the gamut of emotions: relief, disbelief, ecstasy, exhaustion, and triumph. The letter was from the Home Secretary. Townsend was granted a reprieve from the gallows.

The old man was transferred from Winson Green prison to Broadmoor hospital for the criminally insane, where he spent the last years of his life in peace and isolation.

THE BODY
IN THE TRUNK

TODAY'S neighbourhood watch schemes set great store by noticing anything slightly amiss in their road. Milkmen have been performing the same unofficial work over many years. Milkman George Rome raised the alarm when an eccentric old lady's milk bottles were still on her doorstep in Maidenhead in 1948. What was discovered was to horrify the neighbourhood.

Mrs Minnie Freeman Lee was 88 years old, a recluse, and more than a little eccentric. Milkman George Rome knew her strange little ways, and he was used to seeing her out and about, in her old-fashioned black clothes, walking slowly to the shop with her walking stick. She would buy 40 cigarettes every day, and walk home slowly to enjoy a smoke in the one room of the house which was still habitable. All the rest were stuffed with junk. It hadn't always been junk, but when you pile antique furniture up to the ceiling and the roof leaks, it soon disintegrates. Mr Rome left his milk crate on the step and went to the house next door in Ray Park Avenue. It was a fine spring day, and he found neighbour Arthur Hilsdon working on a caravan. He told him of his fears and the two men went back next door. Mr Hilsdon got in through an upstairs window and looked through the house as thoroughly as he could. Some of the doors to the 17 rooms were locked, others were piled so high with discarded furniture that the doors would not open. He came out to join Mr Rome on the front doorstep, shaking his head. On the floor of the hallway was a black court shoe and a bunch of keys, but no sign of the old lady. Hilsdon and Rome thought the best thing to do was to call the police, and before long, PC George Langton arrived. He repeated Mr Hilsdon's search, but without success. 'I cannot find her,' he said as he came out of the front door.

By now, the Magistrates' Clerk had arrived. Mr Kenneth Ruffe Thomas had been legal adviser to Mrs Minnie Freeman Lee for many years, ever since he was a young solicitor in private practice. He lived nearby in Ray Park Avenue.

He went into 'Wynford', Mrs Freeman Lee's home for many years, accompanied by PC Langton. They searched the house again, but found nothing. Mr Thomas saw an old cabin trunk at the side of the hallway. Curiosity drew him to it like a magnet. He undid the straps that held down the lid and unclipped the hasp. It was not locked. The lid was heavy, he could hardly lift it. He raised it to be faced with a sight that made his blood run cold. Inside was the body of Mrs Minnie Freeman Lee. She had been tied up and gagged and had been dead for days. The old lady would have been too weak to scream for help, or put up any sort of a fight against her attacker. But her brutal killer had beaten her about the head, tied her hands behind her back with a woollen shawl and gagged her with a towel before dumping her in the trunk to die of suffocation.

Deeply shocked, Mr Thomas shouted hoarsely for PC Langton. The two men stood in stunned silence at the horror before them. PC Langton went for assistance, and it was not long before more police arrived to cordon off the area and start a detailed search for clues. Detective Superintendent W J Crombie, based at Reading, took charge of the investigation, assisted by Superintendent W H Benstead from Maidenhead.

The whole town was stunned by Mrs Lee's murder. She was a well-known figure locally, regarded as a very wealthy woman, but somewhat odd in her habits. She was the widow of a barrister, and had been a celebrated Victorian beauty. She had come to Maidenhead soon after the turn of the century and was famous for her elegant parties. She used to spend her winters in the south of France or Italy. Sometimes she would stay in Monte Carlo, or at her flat in London. The house was beautifully furnished and she led an enviable lifestyle. Her husband had been dead many years, and she lost her son in the First World War. His death affected her very badly, and gradually she began to withdraw from society, ending up as a virtual recluse.

Despite that, she was still a familiar figure, and even shortly before her death, would walk into town with her walking stick, and often took a taxi home. She had suffered a stroke some time previously, which left her hand withered and made walking difficult. She lived in much reduced circumstances in her old age, and rumours of vast wealth hidden in the house turned out to be fantasy. The only evidence the police could find of any income was £6 a week from a legal benevolent society. She lived in a little world of her own, where her memories meant more to her than the dilapidated house falling down round her ears, and the once expensive furniture was piled high and left to rot in rooms which she never used.

Friends tried to persuade her to sell up and go into a home, where she would be properly looked after. She refused, and clung doggedly to her independence. The WRVS meals on wheels service called regularly at the house, and even up to her last days she was a regular customer for lunch at the Thames Hotel.

House to house enquiries by police led to a host of rumours. A dark, foreign looking man had been seen near the house, and a taxi driver told police he had picked up a man answering that description from the station and taken him to the old lady's house. A shabbily dressed man and woman were seen in Ray Park Avenue. They were reported as singing hymns in the street. Mrs Lee had advertised for a home help shortly before her death. Police appealed for anyone who had responded to the advert.

By now, Detective Superintendent Crombie had called in Scotland Yard. A team of specialist officers, led by Superintendent William Chapman, head of the Flying Squad, arrived at Maidenhead and went through the house with a fine-tooth comb. Superintendent Frederick Cherrill, the Yard's fingerprint expert, arrived at the house and got to work.

Cherrill took off his hat and coat, rolled up his sleeves and went through the house on his hands and knees. His search was minute and painstaking – and effective. Mrs Lee's makeshift bed was in the corner of the downstairs room she lived in. On it was a small cardboard box in which she had kept some jewellery. Cherrill brushed it with finger-print dust, and found two clear finger-prints. They belonged to a man with previous convictions for theft, an itinerant Irishman called George Russell.

Within a week of the trunk being opened, Russell was in custody. He appeared before Maidenhead magistrates and was remanded in custody for a week, charged with murder. Russell, aged 45, was a vagrant who would take whatever work suited him, including a bit of gardening. He was arrested at a hostel in St Albans and taken to Maidenhead police station. He admitted going to look at the garden at Mrs Lee's house, but decided the overgrown jungle there looked too much like hard work. He denied killing Mrs Freeman Lee, but was in possession of a blue silk scarf, similar to one belonging to her, when he was arrested. Russell claimed he bought it for a shilling from a man in London, but the detectives did not believe him.

They took him back to the scene of the crime. 'Have you ever been inside that house?' asked Superintendent Chapman. 'No sir,' replied Russell, and burst into tears.

He was committed for trial and remanded at Oxford Prison to appear before the Assize Court at Reading in

Maidenhead Magistrates Court where George Russell was charged with the murder of an elderly recluse (photograph by Peter Bloodworth).

October, 1948. He denied murdering Mrs Lee, and the evidence given by the Crown rested heavily on the two fingerprints found on the jewellery box. The prosecution claimed Russell had got into the house with the intention of stealing whatever he could. When Mrs Lee disturbed him, he hit her on the head, tied her up, threw her in the trunk and left her to die.

'Did I murder this poor, aged woman for something she was supposed to have, but had not?' said Russell to the jury. 'No. I did not figure in such a murder.'

The court heard that Russell never even knew his parents and had spent his whole life as a vagrant, wandering from town to town. He had spent some weeks earlier in the year working as a kitchen porter at a Maidenhead hotel. He was well known to the police. The judge, Mr Justice Hallett, gave a lengthy summing up, 'If the intruder, who had got into these premises for the purpose of stealing, used violence on this old woman from which she was likely to die, and did die, there can be no question that where the conduct of that intruder resulted in her death, it amounted in point of law to murder.'

Dealing with the question of Russell's credibility, the judge was quite forthright. 'Don't be mealy-mouthed in a criminal case,' he said sternly. 'You have to take your choice on a question of credibility between believing that Russell has lied, or that Superintendent Chapman and his colleagues have told a series of very wicked lies. You may think this man has been the victim, if he is innocent, of a number of cruel circumstances. He was in the hostel just at the wrong time, and bought just the wrong thing – the scarf, and on a box in Mrs Lee's room there were not one, but two fingerprints – one on the top of the lid and one on the side – which Superintendent Cherrill says without the slightest doubt are the fingerprints of this man.'

The jury of ten men and two women took less than two hours to reach a verdict. They went back into the hushed courtroom to be asked 'Do you find the prisoner guilty, or not guilty?' The foreman, Mr J Wolfe-Barry, of the parish of Bray, replied in a firm, clear voice, 'Guilty'.

A nervous half-smile lingered on Russell's face as the judge put on the black cap. 'George Russell, after a most careful and prolonged inquiry, the jury have found you guilty of an offence for which only one sentence is known in our law,' said the judge. 'The sentence of this court is that you be taken from this place to a lawful prison and thence to a place of execution; that you there suffer death by hanging and that your body be afterwards buried in the precincts of the prison, and may the Lord have mercy on your soul.'

Russell's appeal was turned down by the Appeal Court in November, and the Home Secretary, Mr Chuter Ede, announced there were no grounds for a reprieve. On December 2, 1948, George Russell was led to the scaffold at Oxford Prison, and was later buried, in accordance with the judge's traditional direction, in the prison yard.

INDEX